REVELATION

Earth's Final Chapter

AL PITTMAN

COPYRIGHT

CONTENTS

INTRODUCTION

"We know most pastors are not teaching prophecy anymore." – Joel Rosenberg[1]

This stunning statement by Joel Rosenberg, an expert on biblical studies and spiritual-political conditions, should give all of us a reason to pause.

We have come a long way, maybe, from 1980 when Hal Lindsay's book, *The Late Great Planet Earth* was named by the New York Times as the bestselling nonfiction book of the previous decade. Not the Christian book of the decade, the nonfiction book of the decade.

How far we have fallen from the days of frequent prophecy conferences, updates, and a nearly churchwide fervency concerning the imminent return of Jesus Christ. Men such as Chuck Smith, Tim LaHaye, and Chuck Missler were household names and frequent visitors to bestsellers lists. Yes, there were volatile disputes over eschatological issues. Whether the rapture was pre-, mid-, or post-tribulation and other topics were all hotly debated. But at least they were discussed prominently.

The *Left Behind* book series sold tens of millions of copies. Sadly, like the cinematic version of *The Late Great Planet Earth*, the *Left Behind* films were awful at every level.

Still, Jesus commanded His church to be on alert for His return.

This is not to imply that prophecy is totally submerged in today's church landscape; there are old-school beacons such as David Jeremiah, Charles Stanley, and Chuck Swindoll. But it has been largely relegated to the sidelines where devotees of various perspectives have narrow conversations without wide distribution.

This is why I was encouraged to prepare and present a 23-week series that traversed Revelation, chapter by chapter. Sequential teaching has fallen out of favor and has even been criticized as a lazy pulpit style. Where, then, is equipping the church with the full counsel of God's Word (Acts 20:27)? How can a Christian compare Scripture with Scripture, rightly dividing it, if such a major subject is ignored or relegated to symbolic stature? This is a grave error of omission on the part of a growing segment of those on the center stage of church communication.

Israel, the rapture, prophetic elements of current events, and the lifeblood of prophecy—the return of Christ—are ignored or underwhelmingly exposited due to being overshadowed by an "encouragement gospel." Yes, the Bible is a vehicle for encouragement, but the main engine should be the comfort of the soon return of Jesus, and the ageless admonition to watch for this return.

"Watch therefore, for you do not know what hour your Lord is coming." (Matthew 24:42)

THE REVELATION OF JESUS CHRIST

Revelation 1

"And why was the book of Revelation written? It was not written primarily, let me assure you, in order that people might be able to work out the date of the end of the world! That is a very grievous misunderstanding of that book. The book of Revelation was written in order that God's people who were passing through terrible persecutions and terrible adversity might be able to go on rejoicing. If your understanding of the book of Revelation does not help you rejoice, you are misunderstanding it." – Martyn Lloyd-Jones[1]

The Revelation of Jesus Christ, which God gave Him to show His servants—things which must shortly take place. And He sent and signified it by His angel to His servant John, who bore witness to the word of God, and to the testimony of Jesus Christ, to all things that he saw. Blessed is he who reads and those who hear the words of this prophecy, and keep those things which are written in it; for the time is near. (Revelation 1:1–3)

Imagine sitting in a movie theater next to someone who has already seen the movie. The whole time, they're alerting you to the outcome of the movie's critical events *before* they take place. No one wants that. When *The Sixth Sense* first came out, lines formed at theaters for the next showing. Between showtimes at one multiplex, a real comedian walked out of the theater and shouted, "Bruce Willis is dead the whole time!" There were some very unhappy folks.

Revelation is like that, except we're all very glad to know the ending. If I could rename the book, I'd call it *Spoiler Alert! We Win!*

Revelation provides the capstone of our Christian faith, giving us confidence that our future is secure. But it does more than that. Revelation describes the culmination of the glory of Jesus, and it is given to us directly by Jesus himself. This book is *His* revelation, and by the way, it is singular. We need to be clear about that because it is often mistakenly referred to as "Revelations."

The book of Revelation is estimated to have been written around 95 AD. In the Greek, the word translated as "revelation" is *apokálypsi*. This is where we get the term *apocalypse*, which means "disclosure, appearing, or coming." The author of the book is the Apostle John, who referred to himself as "that disciple whom Jesus loved" (John 13, 20, 21). John had been exiled to the island of Patmos by the Roman Emperor Domitian (81–96 AD). Patmos was in the Aegean Sea about twenty-five miles off the coast of Asia Minor. There was a small prison on the island and nothing more.

John—now a castaway, isolated from society, and living in relative obscurity—is set to receive the greatest revelation known to mankind. But isn't that just like God? In our own lives when we've been cast away and the world has given up on us, His greatest work is yet to be revealed! God clearly was not finished with John, and God is not finished with you either. My prayer is that as we go through this amazing book, you will be inspired to live more fully for Christ. John shared a similar sentiment when he declared:

Beloved, now we are children of God; and it has not yet been revealed what we shall be, but we know that when He is revealed, we shall be like Him, for we shall see Him as He is. And everyone who has this hope in Him purifies himself, just as He is pure. (1 John 3:2-3)

WE ARE ON THE CLOCK

Scripture reminds us that in the last days, scoffers would arise mocking the promise of Christ's return (2 Peter 3:3-4), just as people mocked Noah's warning of a flood. Of course in the case of Noah, we know how things ended for those who scoffed. The rains came, the ark was sealed, and the mockers perished from the face of the earth! (Genesis 7). It will be the same for those who scoff at the notion of Christ returning. In regard to the timing of His coming, Peter reminds us:

But, beloved, do not forget this one thing, that with the Lord one day is as a thousand years and a thousand years as one day. The Lord is not slack concerning His promise, as some count slackness, but is longsuffering toward us, not willing that any should perish but that all should come to repentance. (2 Peter 3:8)

Notice in Revelation 1:3 that there is a blessing. In fact, the word used here, *makarios*, means "to be supremely blessed," and the blessing is for *all* who read, hear, and keep this prophecy. The book of Revelation is not science fiction. It is not intended to terrify readers and it certainly should not be avoided. To the contrary, there is promise of a built-in benefit from the simple reading of this document. We should certainly take advantage of that promise.

But we shouldn't stop there. We should earnestly study this book and get it into our hearts because Revelation ultimately reminds us: It is not where you've been but where you're going that matters! From our journey through Revelation, we will be encouraged about our future destination as believers. We will also learn fascinating details of the future that are available in no other document on earth.

REVELATION 1:4-6

This letter is for all believers even though it is specifically addressed to the seven churches in Asia Minor, which is modern-day Turkey. Seven is a significant number in Hebrew culture; it speaks of completion or perfection. Some have taken the seven churches in Revelation to represent the seven stages of the church before Christ returns. If that is the case, the last stage—the Laodicean church—is not very promising. An alternative interpretation is that while the seven types of churches detailed here represent the general flow of church history, each church age contains elements of these seven kinds of churches.

In verse 5, we find confidence for our salvation in statements about who Jesus is and what He has done. First, we are reminded of Christ's reputation as a faithful witness. Jesus said to Pilate, "You could have no power at all against Me unless it had been given you from above" (John 19:11). We are also reminded of Christ's work: He washed us in His own blood. We further find security in the motivation behind His work: love (John 3:16). In verse 6, He emphasizes our eternal status: kings and priests. He has taken us from ruin to royalty. "But you are a chosen generation, a royal priesthood, a holy nation, His own special people, that you may proclaim the praises of Him who called you out of darkness into His marvelous light" (1 Peter 2:9).

In verse 7, we find the second advent, or coming, of Christ. He came first as a lamb to die for our sins; the second time He will return to judge the earth like a lion (Revelation 19). "Every eye" will see Him when "lightning flashes from east to west" (Matthew 24:26–27).

John wanted his readers to know he was not a fair-weather companion. He and the other believers of his time had experienced life together in Christ, through the good, the bad, and the ugly. Christians today are often eager, not just to abandon one another, but to shoot our own wounded! What does the "patience of Christ" look like? It looks like this: "who, when He was reviled, did not revile in return; when He suffered, He did not threaten, but committed Himself to Him who judges righteously" (1 Peter 2:23).

In vv.12-18, John has his mind blown. Notice from verse 17, that our flesh has no defense in the presence of His glory. Every knee should bow and every tongue confess that Jesus is Lord! (Philippians 2:10–11). To the redeemed, however, He says, "Do not be afraid." Not even the grave and death can harm you! He holds the key. "But now having been set free from sin, and having become slaves of God, you have your fruit to holiness, and the end, everlasting life. For the wages of sin is death, but the gift of God is eternal life in Christ Jesus our Lord" (Romans 6:22–23).

Regarding verses 19 and 20, it's worth noting that the revelation of Christ here was preceded by the full revelation of God's love on an old rugged cross. That's why He tells John to write the things he has seen. All throughout Scripture, we find that God doesn't want us to fear for our future. Even communion helps us remember not to fear because it reminds us of the cross.

John has also carried this message of encouragement at other times. This same John assured us in 1 John 4:18–19, "There is no fear in love, but perfect love casts out fear because fear involves torment. But he who fears has not been made perfect in love. We love Him because He first loved us." Have you received the full revelation of God's love for you? Rather than making us afraid, this book is meant to stir excitement and wonder about our future with Christ. As Eugene Peterson once wrote, "I read the revelation not to get more information but to revive my imagination." [2]

Another neat thing about the book of Revelation is that it comes with its own natural outline:

THE THINGS WHICH YOU HAVE SEEN

John had seen the person of the Lord Jesus Christ in the flesh. John had the benefit of seeing Jesus on earth both before and after the resurrection. Now he recounts a vision of the glorified Jesus. The Bible is very limited in giving physical descriptions of what Jesus looked like, but here we find a grand and startling exception. While Isaiah 53:2 tells us that the incarnate Messiah was not physically attractive in a way that He would be desired for His appearance, this is not the case in Revelation. The veil of human camouflage is taken away and John reports a magnificent sight: Jesus in his heavenly glory.

THE THINGS WHICH ARE

John wrote these words as the church age was unfolding. In these two chapters, we discover some crucial information—we find out what Jesus thinks of His church. The seven churches addressed here existed at that time, but as mentioned previously, some believe they also represent various church ages throughout history.

THE THINGS WHICH WILL TAKE PLACE AFTER THIS

In these verses, the curtain is pulled back and we get a detailed view of future events. The "best of the best" for mankind is found here. From the rapture, to the end of the curse, to the millennium and beyond, these chapters take the human mind to the edge of our comprehension. Words can scarcely convey what awaits us in God's glorious future.

And so, with that outline in place, we begin a magnificent journey through the final book of the Bible. In the course of this survey, we will find high peaks of glory and depths of evil beyond what we can currently fathom. Mankind will experience global plagues, spiritual superbeings, and even an unthinkable day when suicide will be impossible. Through it all, remember the first words of this book, "This is the Revelation of Jesus Christ."

2

BLESSED FOR SUCCESS PART 1: EPHESUS

Revelation 2-3

"[Ephesus] Sounds like a great church, doesn't it? It was dynamic, dedicated, patient, disciplined and discerning. But Jesus saw past all the pious facade; the church of Ephesus had heart trouble!" – David Jeremiah[1]

"To the angel of the church of Ephesus write, 'These things says He who holds the seven stars in His right hand, who walks in the midst of the seven golden lampstands: "I know your works, your labor, your patience, and that you cannot bear those who are evil. And you have tested those who say they are apostles and are not, and have found them liars; and you have persevered and have patience, and have labored for My name's sake and have not become weary. Nevertheless I have this against you, that you have left your first love. Remember therefore from where you have fallen; repent and do the first works, or else I will come to you quickly and remove your lampstand from its place—unless you repent. But this you have, that you hate the deeds of the Nicolaitans, which I also hate.

"He who has an ear, let him hear what the Spirit says to the churches. To him who overcomes I will give to eat from the tree of life, which is in the midst of the Paradise of God." ' (Revelation 2:1–7)

Many of us are familiar with the 1975 bestselling book, *Dressed for Success.*

Beyond putting the blue power suit into the wardrobes of executives everywhere, this book formalized what wise salespeople already knew: Clothes may not make the man, but they can help a man get in the right door.

Jesus exhorts the seven churches of Asia, not to be dressed for success, but blessed for success.

The reason for His exhortation to these churches is to help them avoid the deceit and contamination of worldly ways. The Lord exposes spiritual fads, carnal practices, and the danger of drifting away from the core motive of love.

EPHESUS

The first church under this heavenly microscope is Ephesus. Ephesus was a port city located on the Aegean Sea. Ephesus was the fourth largest city in the Roman Empire and remains an impressive ruin to this day. Residents of first-century Ephesus celebrated at least fourteen pagan deities. Foremost among them was Diana, and her temple stood among the seven wonders of the ancient world.

Jesus wastes no time getting down to business with the Ephesian church, saying, "I know your works." There will be no religious games played here. Jesus acknowledges not only the Ephesian work ethic but also their patience and their rejection of those who practiced evil. But in spite of all their faithfulness, they had left their first love. Ouch.

Doctrine and diligence are essential, but not complete without love. If the church fails to take its love of Christ into every aspect of ministry, it is doing the right thing for the wrong reason. This is the core of Jesus's complaint to the Ephesians. Just as heart disease is a major medical threat, the heart of the church must pump pure love for Jesus or face blockages that will threaten its health. Compassionately, Jesus issues more than just a complaint. He also offers them a compliment and a cure.

It's interesting that the Lord starts with this particular church. Could His choice to start with them have to do with the problem He addresses? Our love for the Lord is the most essential thing in our life, so it makes sense that He would want to start with that topic.

Jesus is referencing the same truth He outlines in Matthew 22:37, "You shall love the Lord your God with all your heart." This means our love for God must take mastery over our emotions. We do not live by our feelings, we live by faith as we are governed by God's Word and the Holy Spirit.

What do you meditate on? What dominates your mind? Answer those questions and you will discover the foremost priority of your life. That is the point Jesus is driving home to His church in Ephesus. The believers there worked hard and served faithfully, but they faced many challenges—a situation which undoubtedly made it easy for them to drift from their core motivation.

Acts chapter 19 reveals that the apostle Paul faced fierce opposition to his presentation of the gospel in Ephesus. Historians tell us that Ephesus celebrated numerous pagan deities, and the most popular among those was the goddess Diana, also known as

Artemis. She was a mythological deity worshipped by both Romans and Greeks. Diana was the goddess of the hunt, the moon, and the stars—sort of a weird mother nature.

THE DANGER OF DRIFTING

The name *Ephesus* literally means "desirable" but the believers here had lost their desire for the Lord. They replaced their love for the Lord with their labor in the Lord. They were doing a lot of things but slowly moving away from the best thing which is loving Jesus. Please note that we never naturally drift in a positive direction in the Christian life. If we drift, it is either out to sea or onto the rocks of destruction, never toward God's safe harbor. We only get there by living with purpose.

Godly living is intentional living, and there is no easy way to walk the narrow path of Jesus. The Ephesians prove that you can be in love with the things that you do for Jesus and not be in love with Jesus Himself. "I know your works, your labor, your patience, and that you cannot bear those who are evil" (v. 2). The Ephesian church had a leadership screening process that tested those who said they were apostles but were not. Further, they were commended for their patience and perseverance; they had done work in His name and were not weary. This is wonderful praise from on high, but there is more. Jesus said, "I know your works," but He also knows their hearts.

Now comes the complaint.

"Nevertheless I have this against you, that you have left your first love." (Revelation 2:4)

You have done all these things, but you've left your first love. "I have this against you," Jesus said, therefore:

- Remember from where you have fallen
- Repent. Turn from your course of drifting
- Return to your first love
- Repeat your first works

This seemingly simple four-step plan can have a powerful impact on believers at any time of life. At any age or stage, walking through these calls to action from Jesus will put you on the right path. Try this simple plan as needed to help get you back on track.

A quick response of obedience is prescribed for the Ephesians, and the alternative is severe.

"... or else I will come to you quickly and remove your lampstand from its place—unless you repent. But this you have, that you hate the deeds of the Nicolaitans, which I also hate" (v. 5b-6).

The Nicolaitans were an early heretical sect of so-called believers. Their name comes from two Greek words which mean "to conquer" and "the people." This was a group that promoted a hierarchy within the church which basically said some believers are better than others. The Nicolaitans were dividing the body by promoting a kind of spiritual segregation within the church. This is, of course, the complete opposite of what Jesus taught.

And Jesus basically said, "I hate this type of system."

How is the watching world going to believe the message of the gospel, if the church is devouring one another and exhibiting the same sort of power plays that worldly people face every day? That is why the remedy is clear and the required action is immediate.

"Remember therefore from where you have fallen; repent and do the first works" (v. 5a).

The labor of their flesh was no substitute for genuine love for Jesus. Unless you have a genuine love for Jesus you cannot be a light. Without a light, you cannot bring illumination. If you cannot enlighten others, you cannot be a true witness to the world. That's why there is an urgency in the Lord's voice. The lesson for us is this: We must remember our first love. We must repent or face ruin.

In verse 7, Jesus says, "He who has an ear, let him hear what the Spirit says to the churches. To him who overcomes, I will give to eat from the tree of life, which is in the midst of the Paradise of God." What a wonderful promise! Jesus says to those who have overcome, "I will give to eat from the tree of life." We see in His address to the Ephesians that Jesus is deeply and personally concerned for the church. This is why He walks in the midst of it, evaluating, commenting, and correcting. The church today comes under a great deal of criticism both from inside the church and those outside the church. Perhaps we should leave critiquing the church to the One who designed it and died for it.

As we move from the first church in this list of seven, let us remember that these verses have several layers of application. First, these were actual churches that existed in the first century when John received this revelation. Secondly, these churches are representative of various stages in church history. Finally, we can find personal application in each of the evaluations that Jesus gives to His church.

Certainly, the book of Revelation is brimming with astonishing events in the future, but most of all, it is a personal message to each believer. We must allow the Holy Spirit to use these verses as a tool of illumination to reveal the true state of our hearts.

It is time to come home to our first love. Only then will everything else fall into its proper place.

3

BLESSED FOR SUCCESS PART 2: SMYRNA

Revelation 2-3

"Temptation may even be a blessing to a man when it reveals to him his weakness and drives him to the almighty Saviour. Do not be surprised, then, dear child of God, if you are tempted at every step of your earthly journey, and almost beyond endurance, but you will not be tempted beyond what you are able to bear, and with every temptation, there will be a way of escape." – F.B. Meyer[1]

"And to the angel of the church in Smyrna write, 'These things says the First and the Last, who was dead, and came to life:" I know your works, tribulation, and poverty (but you are rich); and I know the blasphemy of those who say they are Jews and are not, but are a synagogue of Satan. "Do not fear any of those things which you are about to suffer. Indeed, the devil is about to throw some of you into prison, that you may be tested, and you will have tribulation ten days. Be faithful until death, and I will give you the crown of life. "He who has an ear, let him hear what the Spirit says to the

churches. He who overcomes shall not be hurt by the second death."
' (Revelation 2:8–11)

We turn our attention now to the Turkish city of Smyrna, one of the principal cities of Roman Asia. Smyrna competed with both Ephesus and Pergamos for the title "First City of Asia."

Smyrna had been granted the Roman honor of housing a grand temple to Emperor Tiberius. For this reason, Smyrna was the center of fanatical emperor worship. The Romans were passionate about worshiping their emperors as God. Clearly, the young church at Smyrna was on a collision course with the powerful cult of emperor worship. History reveals that the church in this city was persecuted more than any other and it's under that backdrop that Jesus addresses them.

THE SIGN OF SUFFERING

Suffering for Christ is a real element of true discipleship. I have discovered suffering is the means by which God often glorifies himself.

First, the believers in Smyrna are reminded of reality, then they are comforted by His knowledge as Jesus begins His message, "And to the angel of the church in Smyrna write, 'These things says the First and the Last, who was dead, and came to life: "I know your works, tribulation, and poverty (but you are rich); and I know the blasphemy of those who say they are Jews and are not, but are a synagogue of Satan'" (vv. 8–9). Smyrna was a brave church that remained faithful to the Lord despite powerful opposition and persecution.

Even today you can visit the town of Smyrna that is now known as Izmir in Turkey. We also know that the word *Smyrna* means "bitter." The Magi brought myrrh to the Christ child as one of their gifts and this burial ointment is a root name for Smyrna. This precious spice is created by crushing the hardened gum resin from a small bushy tree. Myrrh was used extensively in burial rituals due to its pleasing aroma. This gift was a solemn prophecy of the death Jesus would suffer for the sins of mankind.

Interestingly, in a description of Jesus' reigning during His millennial kingdom, Isaiah observes people bringing gifts of both gold and incense (Isaiah 60:6). The missing ingredient will be myrrh because Jesus will not experience suffering and death ever again.

CAESAR WORSHIP

Let's note that by the time the church at Smyrna was born, worship of Caesar was mandatory in the Roman Empire. This was the source of much of the conflict and persecution that is referred to in Jesus' review of the situation in Smyrna. Christians were brutally persecuted if they defied the decree to bow down to Caesar. Believers were tortured and killed if they refused to burn incense in the temple dedicated to Caesar. They met the same fate for refusing to say "Kaiser Kurios" which means "Caesar is Lord."

It is nearly impossible for Christians living in the modern west to imagine the horrors that have been inflicted upon believers through the ages, including the church at Smyrna. The Lord gave this direction in His letter to the churches: First, be brave. Then be faithful even to the point of death. Christians in Smyrna were hated for their faith, and Jesus understood what they were enduring.

Smyrna was one of only two churches who received no complaint as part of their review (Philadelphia was the other). While Jesus offers comfort and compassion, He does not promise deliverance.

He does offer strength to endure and the crown of life to those who suffer for His name.

CROWNS FROM THE KING

The church in Smyrna was offered compassion, comfort, and the promise of eternal life. But God's goodness to them also included another potential reward—the crown of life.

Five heavenly crowns are mentioned in the New Testament that will be awarded to believers. They are the imperishable crown, the crown of rejoicing, the crown of righteousness, the crown of glory, and the crown of life. The Greek word translated "crown" is *stephanos*. Picture a wreath or garland placed on the head of an athlete at an ancient Olympic sporting event—that's a *stephanos*.

Let's look to Scripture for an understanding of biblical crowns in the New Testament.

THE CROWN OF LIFE

"Do not fear any of those things which you are about to suffer. Indeed, the devil is about to throw some of you into prison, that you may be tested, and you will have tribulation ten days. Be faithful until death, and I will give you the crown of life." (Revelation 2:10)

THE IMPERISHABLE CROWN

"Do you not know that those who run in a race all run, but one receives the prize? Run in such a way that you may obtain it. And everyone who competes for the prize is temperate in all things. Now they do it to obtain a perishable crown, but we for an imperishable crown. Therefore I run thus: not with uncertainty. Thus I fight: not as one who beats the air. But I discipline my body and bring it into

subjection, lest, when I have preached to others, I myself should become disqualified." (1 Corinthians 9:24–27)

THE CROWN OF REJOICING

"For what is our hope, or joy, or crown of rejoicing? Is it not even you in the presence of our Lord Jesus Christ at His coming?" (1 Thessalonians 2:19)

THE CROWN OF RIGHTEOUSNESS

"Finally, there is laid up for me the crown of righteousness, which the Lord, the righteous Judge, will give to me on that Day, and not to me only but also to all who have loved His appearing." (2 Timothy 4:8)

THE CROWN OF GLORY

"and when the Chief Shepherd appears, you will receive the crown of glory that does not fade away." (1 Peter 5:4)

DELIVERANCE DENIED

"My grace is sufficient for you" (2 Corinthians 12:9a). That was the response the apostle Paul received when he prayed to be delivered from affliction. Of course, that is not the answer most of us want when we face some kind of suffering. This often leads to the troubling question: Why? Why can't an all-powerful, loving God simply snap His fingers and solve my crisis? We know He can, but why won't He?

Think about walking into a movie theater well after the film has started. It is frustrating because we have missed so much of the screenplay. Who are the characters? Where are they? Was there a flashback? It is easy to spend the whole movie experience struggling to understand the story. The same can be true for our understanding of God. We walked in well after the drama began so we missed a great deal.

That is why it is crucial for us to thoroughly grasp three principles from the opening of the Bible story.

"In the beginning God created the heavens and the earth. ... And God saw the light, that it was good; and God divided the light from the darkness." (Genesis 1:1, 4)

In this compact cornerstone passage, we learn three critical truths:

- God is—He exists
- God is all-powerful
- God is always good

Unless and until we believe and trust these three points, we will struggle with the story. "How could a loving God...?" When you filter your questions through the fact that God exists, He is omnipotent, and He is good, doubt begins to vanish. Instead, you start to grasp the grand nature of His romance toward humanity— a romance of redemption. A marriage counselor once said, "The Bible begins with a blind date and ends with a splendid wedding!" We can trust that the 'divine wedding planner' has all of the details under control.

THE FOURTH QUARTER

Just over 20 years after Jesus ascended into heaven from the Mount of Olives, parts of His church were already in disarray. In Corinth, the church had become a carnival of carnality, greatly vexing the Apostle Paul. Meanwhile in Galatia, Paul was astonished at how soon the church was bewitched by a grievous error of twisted teaching.

"This was a convoluted, adulterated, corrupted gospel. They were adding works to grace and works to faith. Paul is so exercised about this that there is not at the beginning of this letter any commendation." – John MacArthur [2]

Paul was so worked up that he wrote the following:

O foolish Galatians! Who has bewitched you that you should not obey the truth, before whose eyes Jesus Christ was clearly portrayed among you as crucified? This only I want to learn from you: Did you receive the Spirit by the works of the law, or by the hearing of faith? Are you so foolish? Having begun in the Spirit, are you now being made perfect by the flesh? (Galatians 3:1–3)

By the time John got through his postcards from heaven about the condition of the church, five of the seven had received significantly critical reviews from Jesus.

To summarize the key point about Smyrna, it is totally unrealistic to expect to live a Christian life without opposition, suffering, rejection, and even outright persecution. They hated Him, and they will hate us. These words written to the church in Smyrna are not some divine pep talk; they are firmly based on four attributes of Jesus that will help them endure.

First the authority of Jesus; He is the first and the last, who was dead, and came to life. Those are excellent credentials. John wanted his readers to have confidence that he was delivering a message stamped with the divine authority of a resurrected Christ.

Secondly, they were to be comforted by the total knowledge that Jesus enjoys. His knowledge should be a source of comfort for all who are going through various stages of trials and tribulation. God knows. Cast your cares upon the Lord because He cares for you. Remember, the just shall live by faith. We embrace the rest God gives us through the finished work of the cross. Yes, the gospel is a strong tower. The righteous run to it and they are saved.

Finally, we are comforted by the sovereignty of God. Certainly, the Lord knows everything, but much of it He simply cannot tell us at this time due to our human frailty and limited capacity. Someone said God always precedes—He always goes before us.

I am in the fourth quarter of my life. I recognize that as always, I must be redeeming the time in this season. We need to ignore the siren call of the world that encourages us to check off our bucket list of exotic events before our bodies finally betray us. Like the Christian church in Smyrna, we must look over the horizon of this fallen world for a day when the curse is removed, every tear is wiped away, and death is no more. Then, my friends, it all begins.

4

BLESSED FOR SUCCESS PART 3: PERGAMOS

Revelation 2-3

"Beyond all the other sites in Asia Minor, it gives the traveler the impression of a royal city, the home of authority. The rocky hill on which it stands is so huge, it dominates the broad plain of the Caucasus River Valley so proudly and so boldly." – Sir William Ramsay, 19th-century archaeologist[1]

"And to the angel of the church in Pergamos write, 'These things says He who has the sharp two-edged sword: "I know your works, and where you dwell, where Satan's throne is. And you hold fast to My name, and did not deny My faith even in the days in which Antipas was My faithful martyr, who was killed among you, where Satan dwells. But I have a few things against you, because you have there those who hold the doctrine of Balaam, who taught Balak to put a stumbling block before the children of Israel, to eat things sacrificed to idols, and to commit sexual immorality. Thus you also have those who hold the doctrine of the Nicolaitans, which thing I

hate. Repent, or else I will come to you quickly and will fight against them with the sword of My mouth.

"He who has an ear, let him hear what the Spirit says to the churches. To him who overcomes I will give some of the hidden manna to eat. And I will give him a white stone, and on the stone a new name written which no one knows except him who receives it." ' (Revelation 2:12–17)

The third church letter we come to is addressed to the church at Pergamos. This city was 100 miles north of Ephesus in the area called Asia Minor. It was 15 miles inland from the Aegean Sea. It was not on any major trade route nor was it a port city. Pergamos did have a massive library because it was an important center for education and culture and an important center of pagan worship.

There were a number of deities that were typically honored in a Roman-era city of this type. The Romans and Greeks were generous in their rampant idolatry, but one idol loomed above all the rest in Pergamos, and that was Athena. A massive statue of Athena loomed over the city. But Athena was not alone. Down below in the heart of the city, affections were divided between Zeus and the emperor cult, which at that time centered around Emperor Domitian.

Where Jesus refers to the "throne of Satan," there is actually controversy over which form of idolatry He was addressing. In any case, there was also a huge healing center in Pergamos that was popular both with locals and travelers. The god Asclepius could supposedly heal people from all their diseases. Asclepius was depicted as a nonpoisonous snake in his temple. Nonpoisonous snakes slithered all over the floor of the temple. It must have been a wild waiting room because if you wanted to be healed, the prescribed method was to come to the temple and lay down on the floor, letting the snakes crawl all over you. Sounds like the cure was worse than the disease!

Remember, Revelation 12:9 calls Satan "the great dragon, the serpent," and he is slithering around the world today. Yes, his days are numbered. His fate is certain and final, but for now we must be sober and vigilant.

The name *Pergamos* means "marriage." Sadly, Jesus warns the believers in this city that they are unfaithful. They are pursuing a different love. Idolatry is the act of placing anything or anyone above God. Pergamos was clearly living in dangerous circumstances and their response was to live a compromised life. Jesus acknowledges their environment but sharply warns about the consequences of compromise.

Billy Graham said, "The very ones whose social pressure cause you to compromise will despise you for it. They probably respect your convictions, and many of them wish they had the moral stamina to stand alone."[2] He also said, "Be attractive and winsome, but do not compromise your convictions for the sake of popularity." [3]

COMPROMISED CHRISTIANS

In the shadow of this vibrant culture of idolatry, it is no wonder that the church was conflicted by compromise. Powerful pressures were exerted on all Roman citizens to honor and worship their emperor. We can also easily imagine the peer and commercial pressure that Christians came under.

What if a believer worked for a strong Roman who frequently gave incense and honored Caesar? If their Christian convictions prevented them from following suit, it could have easily cost them their job and perhaps much more. It could have cost them their life, as it did Antipas.

What pressures are you under in your spiritual life? In the west physical persecution is relatively rare, but social and cultural forces are commonly exerted on Christians who are open about their beliefs. The Christian faith is portrayed as outdated, ancient, and even dangerous in the media and public square of America. And keep in mind that the violent persecution first-century believers often encountered is a constant threat in many parts of the world today.

In fact, monitoring organizations report that in many parts of Asia and Africa, the 20th century was one of the most dangerous in church history.

Open Doors USA reports that around the world, more than 260 million Christians live in places where they experience high levels of persecution. That's one out of every nine believers worldwide. Open Doors also reports the following statistics:

- 2,983 Christians killed for their faith
- 9,488 churches and other Christian buildings were attacked.
- 3,711 believers detained without trial, arrested, sentenced, or imprisoned[4]

Here are some modern-day stories from Christians who are just like you except for where they live.

"It is unnatural—maybe even wrong—to keep one's love for Jesus entirely to oneself. I cannot tell my wife. Or my children. Or my parents. I found Christ in a dream, and only He knows I follow him. But I have to, or I'm dead. ... It's too risky. If the authorities find a Christian Bible on my person, they will interrogate me, and I will not lie, so my new faith would be exposed. I do not know how long I can go without fellowship, without witness, living a lie." – Quote from an unnamed Saudi Christian

In Syria, a Christian pastor who is unnamed for security reasons reports that despite regular bombings and a dark and dangerous environment, his church has recently grown from 100 to 500.

"The Church is the source of joy because Jesus stayed on the cross and Syria is on the cross and awaiting the day it will be resurrected. No one in any society has this joy except the Church. ... We are not passing through anything our Lord did not pass through himself and triumph over. Being persecuted recently in Syria is nothing. We have been persecuted for centuries, and it does not hurt the Church but serves it." – Quote from an unnamed Syrian pastor[5]

It is important that we do not view the church through a strictly American lens. When other parts of the body of Christ suffer, we should share their pain by praying, giving, and going to where they are.

"And if one member suffers, all the members suffer with it; or if one member is honored, all the members rejoice with it." (1 Corinthians 12:26)

WICKED TRIFECTA: COMPROMISE, IDOLATRY, & IMMORALITY

The poison that Jesus identified in the body at Pergamos also included sexual immorality. To illustrate, this letter points out the doctrine of Balaam that thrived in the shadow of this throne of Satan. Sexual intercourse was a part of the worship ceremony for the pagan god Baal, who was among the pantheon of idols in the Roman world. Satan, the ultimate liar, has been wildly successful with sexual propaganda.

So-called "free love" which permeated the 1960s was merely an echo of the lies told throughout the ages. Why should Satan change the bait when it has worked so well in hooking foolish followers of unbridled sex? Bodies, families, and testimonies have all been ruined by falling prey to this lie of sexual fulfillment outside of marriage.

The Lord's solution to compromise, idolatry, and immorality is simple: "Repent." Turn from your sin and enjoy the twofold benefit we find here. First, the Lord rewards the faithful with hidden manna (v. 17), which refers to the bread of life sent from God in the person of Jesus Christ. He is our portion and nourishment to our soul. This manna is hidden from those who live in unbelief, but it is freely given to the children of God.

Second, He offers a white stone and a new name (v. 17). The white stone may be an allusion to the Old Testament practice of the high priest wearing 12 stones on his breastplate. In this case, the white stone represented purity through repentance from immorality. Along with the stone, the repentant person is promised a new name, which speaks to the promise that a Christian is a new creation, has a new identity, and can now relate to God personally and intimately through Jesus Christ.

Therefore "Come out from among them and be separate, says the Lord. Do not touch what is unclean, And I will receive you. I will be a Father to you, and you shall be My sons and daughters, Says the LORD Almighty." (2 Corinthians 6:17–18)

It is time to come out from among the shadows and into the light. This is the road to being blessed for success.

5

BLESSED FOR SUCCESS PART 4: THYATIRA

Revelation 2-3

"Sexual contact between a boy and a girl is a progressive thing. In other words, the amount of touching and caressing and kissing that occurs in the early days tends to increase as they become more familiar and at ease with one another. Likewise, the amount of contact necessary to excite one another increases day by day, leading in many cases to an ultimate act of sin and its inevitable consequence. This progression must be consciously resisted by Christian young people who want to serve God and live by His standards. They can resist this trend by placing deliberate controls on the physical aspect of their relationship, right from the first date." – James C. Dobson[1]

"And to the angel of the church in Thyatira write, 'These things says the Son of God, who has eyes like a flame of fire, and His feet like fine brass: "I know your works, love, service, faith, and your patience; and as for your works, the last are more than the first.

Nevertheless I have a few things against you, because you allow that woman Jezebel, who calls herself a prophetess, to teach and seduce My servants to commit sexual immorality and eat things sacrificed to idols. And I gave her time to repent of her sexual immorality, and she did not repent. Indeed I will cast her into a sickbed, and those who commit adultery with her into great tribulation, unless they repent of their deeds. I will kill her children with death, and all the churches shall know that I am He who searches the minds and hearts. And I will give to each one of you according to your works.

"Now to you I say, and to the rest in Thyatira, as many as do not have this doctrine, who have not known the depths of Satan, as they say, I will put on you no other burden. But hold fast what you have till I come. And he who overcomes, and keeps My works until the end, to him I will give power over the nations—

'He shall rule them with a rod of iron;

They shall be dashed to pieces like the potter's vessels'—

as I also have received from My Father; and I will give him the morning star.

"He who has an ear, let him hear what the Spirit says to the churches." ' (Revelation 2:18–29)

Jesus' fourth letter is to the church of Thyatira, where He addresses the issue of sexual immorality. We may well wonder, "Didn't the Lord address this issue in His letter to the Church in Pergamos?" Yes. However, there's a difference. What Pergamos tolerated, Thyatira fully embraced.

We live in a society today which has also largely embraced sexual immorality. Consider the following statistics from PureHope.net.[2]

- Sex is the #1 topic people search for on the internet
- There are over 420 million pornographic internet pages
- 12 to 17-year-olds are the largest consumers of internet pornography
- Porn is estimated to be a $97 billion industry, with $12 billion of that in the U.S.
- 624,000 child porn traders have been discovered in the U.S.
- 50% of all Christian men and 20% of all Christian women are addicted to pornography.
- 5 out of 10 pastors struggle with temptations to view pornography.

But there is hope in Christ, so this letter to Thyatira is not one of condemnation. Rather, it's a message of liberation.

"He who sins is of the devil, for the devil has sinned from the beginning. For this purpose the Son of God was manifested, that He might destroy the works of the devil." (1 John 3:8)

THE CAUSE

First, the Lord establishes His right as the only true authority in His church. He sees all as He walks among His people.

Joseph Seiss, a 19th-century theologian writes, "There is nothing more piercing than flaming fire. Everything yields and melts before it. It penetrates all things, consumes every opposition, sweeps down all obstructions, and presses its way with invincible power. And of this sort are the eyes of Jesus. They look through everything; they pierce through all masks and coverings; they search the remotest recesses; they behold the most hidden things of the soul; and there is no escape from them. As the Son of God, He is omniscient as well as mighty."[3]

His feet of brass come into view next, representing that Jesus enjoys full access into all church proceedings. No area is beyond His scrutiny. No security person prevents Jesus from going backstage, into the green room, or checking out the church business office.

The underlying cause of the problems at Thyatira was false teaching. Jesus calls this false teaching the doctrine of Jezebel. The woman Jezebel, described to us in the Old Testament, was the personification of evil. She was the wicked wife of King Ahab who reigned in northern Israel (1 Kings 16:29). Jezebel actively promoted the worship of Baal, the pagan Canaanite God. Worship of Baal included ritual acts of perversion and sensuality. Within the church at Thyatira, a woman in the pattern of Jezebel, a self-appointed prophetess, was being allowed to seduce others into embracing sexual immorality.

In this city, the Greek god Apollo was worshiped and highly revered. Apollo represented a blend of different religious beliefs and practices. In Luke 16:15, Jesus warned, "You are those who justify yourselves before men, but God knows your hearts. For what is highly esteemed among men is an abomination in the sight of God."

Bible historians tell us that trade guilds (unions) were plentiful in this city. These groups were known to hold banquets in the halls of pagan temples. After the formalities, the night would often degenerate into an evening of debauchery. In order to get along and not lose their career status, many believers were inclined to go along with these perverted events.

Today, many believers participate in sexual immorality on a regular basis in the name of grace, but in reality they are being seduced by a Jezebel spirit. Remember the words of the apostle Paul:

"You cannot drink the cup of the Lord and the cup of demons; you cannot partake of the Lord's table and of the table of demons. Or do we provoke the Lord to jealousy? Are we stronger than He?" (1 Corinthians 10:21–22)

This wicked woman in Thyatira refused mercy and stiffened her heart to repentance. Consequently, she opened the door to a fate that was similar to the fate of her namesake, who was murdered and eaten by dogs (2 Kings 9:36–37). Sexual immorality is a great deceiver. Thus, we must yield our heart to constant examination by the Holy Spirit. We should allow Him to frequently check whether we have allowed evil to reside in our holy of holies.

"Search me, O God, and know my heart; Try me, and know my anxieties; And see if there is any wicked way in me and lead me in the way everlasting." (Psalm 139:23–24)

THE CURE

Now we come to the cure (vv. 24–25). "Hang on" is basically the advice given to those who seek the knowledge of Christ rather than the depths of Satan. To escape sexual sin, we must upset old carnal patterns in our lives. Our regular spiritual patterns of Bible study, prayer, fellowship, and service must be paired with active repentance of any sin God reveals to us. In order to avoid the setup of Satan, we must upset patterns of sin in our lives. One way to do this is to regularly and intentionally establish new positive habits in our daily routine.

"Every action you take is a vote for the type of person you wish to become. No single instance will transform your beliefs, but as the votes build up, so does the evidence of your new identity." – James Clear[4]

SATANIC STRATEGY

Try to imagine yourself playing chess against Satan. How do you think that would go? Would your strategy match his? I think not! Even a grandmaster would wither going one on one in this situation. This opponent has supernatural skills and thousands of years of experience. He knows how to probe for his opponent's weakness.

Do you realize that Satan has a strategy for attacking your life? First, he has a generic plan for the entire human race utilizing the big three: lust of the eyes, lust of the flesh, and pride of life (1 John 2:16).

Beyond this general approach, the forces of evil have examined you individually and developed a personalized plan to discourage you, depress you, and defeat your efforts for the gospel. Remember the words of Jesus to Peter in Luke 22:31, "Simon, Simon! Indeed, Satan has asked for you, that he may sift you as wheat." I suppose Peter panicked before Jesus completed His thought, "But I have prayed for you, that your faith should not fail" (Luke 22:32a).

Here is a thoughtful observation from John Stott about the strategies of Satan, "If the devil cannot conquer the church by the application of political pressure or the propagation of intellectual heresy, he will try the insinuation of moral evil. This was the dragon's strategy in Thyatira."[5]

6

BLESSED FOR SUCCESS PART 5: SARDIS

Revelation 2-3

"The early church was strikingly different from the culture around it in this way—the pagan society was stingy with its money and promiscuous with its body. A pagan gave nobody their money and practically gave everybody their body. And the Christians came along and gave practically nobody their body and they gave practically everybody their money."— Timothy Keller[1]

"And to the angel of the church in Sardis write, 'These things says He who has the seven Spirits of God and the seven stars: "I know your works, that you have a name that you are alive, but you are dead... You have a few names even in Sardis who have not defiled their garments; and they shall walk with Me in white, for they are worthy." (Revelation 3:1, 4)

In His fifth letter to the seven churches in Asia, Jesus addresses the church in Sardis, which was a prosperous city. In fact it was considered to be among the wealthiest areas in the world. The church in America needs to hear and heed this important message. Just as in first-century Smyrna, we are surrounded by an affluent society and all of the temptations that go along with it.

ROCKING CHURCH

The church in Sardis had a reputation for being a lively fellowship. Music was top-notch, celebrities spoke well of them, and they were solid financially. This church had it going on. The only problem? They were dead. Now that is a serious problem to have.

A.W. Tozer once said, "If the Holy Spirit was withdrawn from the church today, ninety-five percent of what we do would go on and no one would know the difference."[2]

We have learned to do church very well today, but we need more than slick PowerPoint presentations. We need the power of the Holy Spirit.

As Zechariah reminds us, "Not by might, nor by power, but by My Spirit," says the Lord of hosts (Zechariah 4:6b).

DEAD CHURCH

The words written to Sardis are the harshest on the list. Where did they go wrong? In verse 2, we find they had stopped being watchful. They had also ceased exercising their faith, as evidenced by their lack of good works. Prayer is the obvious means to remain alert. It keeps us aware of our spiritual surroundings and heart condition.

There is no compliment to be found from Jesus concerning His church in Sardis. This was one cold, dead church.

Recall that for the Ephesus, Pergamos, and Thyatira churches, Jesus had a combination of praise and rebuke. Smyrna received nothing but compliments, but Sardis is exactly the opposite. While Jesus notes that a few individuals in Sardis "have not defiled their garments," He has nothing commendable to say about the church itself. This is mildly surprising since the Sardis church had a good reputation. However, their reputation was without factual basis—they had a nice facade but no function.

However, graciously following the complaint of Jesus, we come to the cure.

Strengthen what remains (v. 2) is a great word of encouragement. It is totally unproductive to spend your life lamenting over the bad choices in your past. Here is some wisdom: Stop cheating on your future with your past—it is over.

To press on is to remain watchful, strengthening our faith, so we do not become spiritual zombies. To avoid a zombie-like faith, we must start where faith begins and that is hearing and receiving the truth.

To strengthen the things that remain in your life, you need to identify the foundation of your faith. What do you believe? Storms may damage some of the cosmetics of our life, but a firm foundation remains undisturbed.

The call here is to cling to the cornerstone because we never outgrow the basics of our faith.

TREMBLING AT THE WORD

Here is some insight from the book of Isaiah, "But on this one will I look: On him who is poor and of a contrite spirit, and who trembles at My word" (Isaiah 66:2b).

The effectiveness of God's word is directly connected to how we hear it, receive it, and apply it. If you are looking for evidence of your true spiritual condition, look back over the path of your recent past. You should observe three things: points of repentance, signs of goodness, and signs of mercy.

Famously, David wrote in Psalm 23:6, "Surely, goodness and mercy will follow me all the days of my life."

To walk with Jesus in a worthy manner is to live carefully knowing that every trial, and even our failures, are an opportunity for progress in Jesus. Never lose your high regard for the word of God. It must be honored, respected, and obeyed.

THE BOOK OF LIFE

Much has been made about verse 5 and the promise to retain names in the Book of Life. Some contend this suggests the possibility of losing the promise of salvation, when in fact, it teaches just the opposite. Believers are assured they have a permanent place on the role call of eternal life. As one commentator observed, "God does not write in the Book of Life in pencil."

One suggested solution to the supposed problem is that there is a master book of the living where names are removed at the point of physical death. However, when properly understood, this passage reveals that the Book of Life is a list of those who have gained eternal life through Jesus Christ. This is the promise given to the faithful few at Sardis.

LIMITING THE HOLY ONE

It is astonishing to comprehend that a mere mortal man has been granted the ability to frustrate God.

"Again and again they put God to the test; they vexed the Holy One of Israel." (Psalm 78:41 NIV)

Another version is more pointed, saying Israel 'limited' the Holy One. Yes, again and again they tempted God when they did not remember His power. Our carnal affections for sensual things limit God's work in our lives. It is high time that we stop living like zombies. Jesus calls us to be alert and to strengthen the things that remain.

7

BLESSED FOR SUCCESS PART 6: PHILADELPHIA

Revelation 2-3

"The deepest thought a person can ever have is his conception of God's character." – Dan DeHaan[1]

"And to the angel of the church in Philadelphia write, 'These things says He who is holy, He who is true, He who has the key of David, He who opens and no one shuts, and shuts and no one opens: I know your works. See, I have set before you an open door, and no one can shut it; for you have a little strength, have kept My word, and have not denied My name. Indeed I will make those of the synagogue of Satan, who say they are Jews and are not, but lie— indeed I will make them come and worship before your feet, and to know that I have loved you. Because you have kept My command to persevere, I also will keep you from the hour of trial which shall come upon the whole world, to test those who dwell on the earth. Behold, I am coming quickly! Hold fast what you have, that no one may take your crown. He who overcomes, I will make him a pillar in the temple of My God, and he shall go out no more. I will write

on him the name of My God and the name of the city of My God, the New Jerusalem, which comes down out of heaven from My God. And I will write on him My new name.

"He who has an ear, let him hear what the Spirit says to the churches." ' (Revelation 3:7–13)

We now come to the church at Philadelphia, considered by some to be the most attractive of the seven. This letter may be the most important of the seven because it reveals a dependence upon Christ, which was generally missing from the other churches. Philadelphia is also one of only two churches that Jesus praised without issuing any complaint. Neither Philadelphia nor Smyrna was great and powerful; both were small and weak, yet endorsed by Jesus.

What made the church in Philadelphia distinct? History shows that the surrounding environment was ungodly, just as it was for the other churches. The believers in Philadelphia also suffered rejection and persecution. The faithfulness of this church was not due to the absence of worldly culture and godless influence. Instead, their faithfulness was proven in spite of those things.

As in other letters, Jesus establishes His sovereign authority; it is Jesus alone who possesses the character and conduct worthy of commending the church. Jesus also holds the key of David which further endorses His holy authority (v. 7). The lesson is that God alone opens one door and closes another. Here the door speaks of opportunity, and as we learn from 1 Corinthians 16:9, effective ministry often comes with significant adversity: "For a great and effective door has opened to me, and there are many adversaries."

CHURCH OF THE OPEN DOOR

We might call Philadelphia the missionary church because their door was wide open to all. This has not always been true of the church throughout the centuries.

Sadly, the spirit of legalism, strange doctrines, and even racial segregation has shut the church door in the face of many. Clearly, this is not a reflection of God's heart or will. Jesus said, "Go into all the world and preach the gospel" (Mark 16:15). That is a very inclusive command. In some eras, the church has stepped up to this challenge.

"In church history, the period of the great missionary outreach, from 1750 until around 1925, was exemplified by the church of Philadelphia. This was the era of Hudson Taylor, D.L. Moody, and many more. The Salvation Army was founded; a whole galaxy of home missionary agencies sprung up. It was a time of great spiritual awakening." – David Jeremiah[2]

CITY OF BROTHERLY LOVE

Philadelphia was also referred to as "Little Athens" because of the pagan temples and public buildings that populated the city. Philadelphia is categorized as the church of the open door. This indicates that Philadelphia was active in evangelism and that they welcomed all interested persons.

In verse 8 Jesus gives what might be considered a mixed blessing when He says, "You have a little strength." Weakness is not a detriment if it leads to depending on a source of power.

That is what Paul recognized when he wrote, "And He said to me, 'My grace is sufficient for you, for My strength is made perfect in weakness.' Therefore most gladly I will rather boast in my infirmities, that the power of Christ may rest upon me" (2 Corinthians 12:9).

It is important to note that the door set before this church was not based on their strength—they only had a little strength. Jesus was looking for their availability, not their ability.

UPSIDE-DOWN KINGDOM

The recognition that weakness can lead to strength is a common theme of the New Testament.

Do you desire to live? God's answer is to die to self. You want to be great in God's kingdom? Learn to be the servant of all. Interested in being wealthy towards God? Give and you will have treasure in heaven. Of course, it is not God's kingdom that is inverted. Jesus came to set the world right side up.

The world we currently inhabit is not a wonderful place, no matter how much we may want it to be. Certainly we still see glimmers of the glories of Genesis, but they are dulled by rebellion, muted by untold generations determined to insult God and elevate fallen man. This rebel planet will not stand. So grievous have the repercussions of the fall of man been, that nothing short of a new heaven and earth will correct what C.S. Lewis called "The Great Divorce."

SYNAGOGUE OF SATAN

In verses 9 and 10, Jesus addresses a certain group of spiritual bullies found in the early church. They were called "Judaizers."

The group was made up of Jews who said they believed the gospel, but in fact they were of the "synagogue of Satan." This was because they promoted another gospel: salvation through the law rather than grace. Therefore, Jesus declared in verse 9 that those who are antagonistic towards believers will eventually have to humble themselves before the true church, acknowledging how much Jesus loves the body at Philadelphia.

THE GREAT TRIBULATION

Endless controversy exists around what takes place surrounding the period known as the great tribulation. This seven-year period is described as the worst time imaginable. One's view of who will be present for this horror and when it will take place in the prophetic timeline is normally determined by whether they subscribe to the pre-, mid-, or post-tribulation view.

The pre-tribulation position is strengthened by this scriptural fact: the church is mentioned several times in the first three chapters of Revelation. From chapter four on, when a "great door is opened in heaven" (4:1), the church is not mentioned again in Revelation. The church is gone.

If you want to start a small riot, take a strong position on the rapture in a diverse group of Christians. I believe the promise that Philadelphia would be delivered from the "hour of tribulation" refers to that seven-year period yet to come, which is described for us in the beginning of Revelation 6. This is one of the reasons why I believe in the pre-tribulation rapture of the church.

A PREVIEW OF GLORY

Whatever your conclusions on the tribulation and the church's role in end time events, this much is indisputable: Jesus encouraged His followers with a glimpse of their glorious future (v. 12). Overcomers are those who have placed their faith and trust in Christ (1 John 5:4-5); they will be a pillar in the temple of God. "Pillar" speaks of a permanent position in heaven. In fact, God Almighty and the Lamb will be the ultimate new temple (Revelation 21:22). Believers will also bear the name of the city of God, that is "New Jerusalem" (Revelation 21:2). Lastly, He will also write on them His "new name" (Revelation 19:12), a name not yet known.

Gospel singer Danniebelle Hall sang the song "Ordinary People" where the last line of the chorus says, "Little becomes much as you place it in the Master's hand!"

God uses ordinary people for his extraordinary purpose and glory.

Just ordinary People

God uses ordinary people

He chooses people just like me and you

Who are willing to do what He commands

God uses people that will give him all

No matter how small your all may seem to you

Because little becomes much as you place it in the Master's hand

(Lyrics from the song "Ordinary People")[3]

8

BLESSED FOR SUCCESS PART 7: LAODICEA

Revelation 2-3

"Lukewarm people don't really want to be saved from their sin; they want only to be saved from the penalty of their sin." – Francis Chan[1]

"And to the angel of the church of the Laodiceans write, 'These things says the Amen, the Faithful and True Witness, the Beginning of the creation of God: I know your works, that you are neither cold nor hot. I could wish you were cold or hot. So then, because you are lukewarm*, and neither cold nor hot, I will vomit you out of My mouth. Because you say, "I am rich, have become wealthy, and have need of nothing"—and do not know that you are wretched, miserable, poor, blind, and naked—I counsel you to buy from Me gold refined in the fire, that you may be rich; and white garments, that you may be clothed, that the shame of your nakedness may not be revealed; and anoint your eyes with salve, that you may see... Behold, I stand at the door and knock. If anyone hears My voice and opens the door, I will come in to him and dine with him, and he*

with Me. To him who overcomes I will grant to sit with Me on My throne, as I also overcame and sat down with My Father on His throne.

'He who has an ear, let him hear what the Spirit says to the churches." ' (Revelation 3:14–18, 20–22)

This is the final of seven churches reviewed by Jesus in this second part of the book of Revelation. We travel now forty-five miles from Philadelphia to the ancient city of Laodicea. In the Lord's final letter, Jesus sternly rebukes this church.

Many believe this letter represents the final stage of the church before the coming of the Lord. Given the fact that we are prophetically in the last days, this letter serves as a possible indictment against today's church.

Once again, in verse 14 the Lord opens His letter with a declaration of divine authority.

LUKEWARM

Neither hot nor cold, but lukewarm. This is the scornful indictment Jesus delivers (v. 15-16). You can almost hear the tinge of sarcasm and disdain in His voice as he delivers this stinging rebuke, but it gets worse.

"Therefore, I will vomit you out of my mouth." How devastating to find that your life nauseates the One you supposedly worship, serve, and obey.

Why would Jesus use such a word? Possibly because of the two sources of water residing north and south of the city. Laodicea was situated between the thermal hot springs of Hierapolis and the cold mountain springs flowing from the south, fed by the snowmelt throughout the year. While coming from a cold source, this fresh water would become lukewarm inside the ceramic pipes used in the Roman water system.[2]

The church had become what is known as an *emetic*, which is a substance that causes vomiting. Their Christian pretense, religiosity, and arrogance made God gag.

Worse, the Laodicean church thought they did not need God (v. 17). This city was located at the intersection of three well-traveled highways. Laodicea was a highly successful commercial and financial center, with an abundance of wealthy bankers and financiers—the Wall Street of its day. The economic prosperity of this city apparently had lulled the church into a sense of false security, resulting in spiritual apostasy.

HOT OR COLD?

The Greek word for hot is *zestos*, meaning "boiling hot." This is the heart of saying someone is "on fire" for the Lord. In Laodicea, the members had lost their enthusiasm, emotion, and zest for the Lord. We live in such a time today in many parts of the church. In Matthew 24:12, Jesus warned of just such a time, "And because lawlessness will abound, the love of many will grow cold."

Our only defense against a hard-hearted faith is maintaining a fervent, white-hot love for Jesus. Can you recall a time when you were more zealous for the Lord than you are now? If so, that should be a yellow flag of caution. If you are not getting hotter, you are getting colder, and that is never a positive.

Do not procrastinate. Immediately identify what has dampened your enthusiasm for the things of the Lord. Throw that impostor out of your life and put more logs on your spiritual fire.

THE GREAT PHYSICIAN AT WORK

The problem for the Laodiceans was that their self-evaluation was the polar opposite of what Jesus saw.

And yet, for each of their carnal conditions (v. 17), Jesus provided a remedy through the counsel of His word (v. 18). Gold here is used as a metaphor for true riches, that which is pure and tried, of eternal value. But the Laodiceans lacked true riches. Not only that, they were in poverty to the point of nakedness. What a bad dream that is! To go through life spiritually naked, but unaware of your true condition would be a nightmare. Jesus offers a new wardrobe to remedy their unrecognized, naked condition.

But the Laodiceans weren't just naked, they were also blind. So the Lord counseled that they should anoint their eyes. Historians say that Laodicea was home to a renowned medical school that developed a popular eye salve called "Phrygian powder." This salve was reputed to cure certain kinds of eye diseases. People came from all over the Roman world in search of remedies for their ailments. How ironic that the church was in a city renowned for healing eye disease and yet they were spiritually blind.

KNOCK KNOCK

Remember that the vision of John began in chapter one with Jesus walking among the seven candlesticks, which represented the seven churches.

By the time He gets to the church at Laodicea He is outside the church, knocking! What an awful and frightening situation. And yet, Jesus graciously indicates His desire to enjoy intimate fellowship and dine with this church. But first, they have to let him in.

Holman Hunt painted a famous scene of Christ knocking at the door, revealing that symbolically there is no latch on the outside. The control lies with those on the inside.

One pastor told the anecdotal story of a poorly dressed woman who was not allowed inside an upscale church. As she mournfully walked down the church steps and came across Jesus, she told Him her story. He comforted her by saying, "Don't feel bad, I can't get inside either."

To be blessed for success has nothing to do with wearing a power suit or any other element of a physical wardrobe. We learn these lessons from the seven churches:

- Love Jesus first. (Ephesus)
- Do not fear. (Smyrna)
- Do not compromise. (Pergamos)
- Avoid sexual immorality. (Thyatira)
- Be watchful and strengthen what remains. (Sardis)
- Be faithful. (Philadelphia)
- Be hot for the Lord. (Laodicea)

This is the proper attire for success in Christ.

9

THE HEAVENLY VISION

Revelation 4-5

"If you read history you will find that the Christians who did the most for the present world were just those who thought most of the next. It is since Christians have largely ceased to think of the other world that they have become so ineffective in this." – C.S. Lewis[1]

After these things I looked, and behold, a door standing open in heaven. And the first voice which I heard was like a trumpet speaking with me, saying, "Come up here, and I will show you things which must take place after this." (Revelation 4:1)

POSTCARDS FROM PARADISE

At one time before Instagram, people on vacation actually bought postcards, signed them, and sent them. Of course, many times they arrived home before the cards were delivered.

In chapters 4 and 5, we find a brilliant glimpse of heaven delivered right on time. Before we take a long look at this celestial message, we must focus on the first verse of chapter 4. This verse is a pivotal point in the unveiling of Jesus Christ and the book of Revelation as a whole.

"After these things," refers to the things of the church. So, after the time of the church, the balance of the veil is gradually pulled to fully reveal Jesus, capturing the wonder and awe of the entire universe. From here on, the church is simply gone, and the world moves forward from bad to worse.

John sees a door and then hears a trumpet—a divine call that comes through loud and clear. The center of this scene is the throne of God, which is mentioned twelve times in the fourth chapter. John, who has been caught up to heaven in this vision, is now granted the highest human privilege possible: he describes the "One" who sat on the throne.

Remember, words are containers to carry meaning, but they have their limits. In this passage, John reaches the height of what language can accomplish, so he does not attempt to describe God's indescribable form.

What we do have in the third verse of chapter 4 is a portrayal of the glory residing on the throne. Two colors radiate from the throne—the colors of jasper and sardius. Both are precious stones that were found in the breastplate of an Old Testament high priest. These stones also can represent God's glory and His righteous government.

THE THRONE ROOM

Around the throne, John sees an emerald rainbow. This rainbow represents God's faithfulness, a sign of promise and hope. In verse

4, encircling the throne are twenty-four other thrones occupied by elders who are representative of Old and New Testament spiritual leaders. They are clothed in perfect white garments and graced with golden crowns that signify their roles as priests and kings.

From the throne came lightning, thundering, and voices rolling out as a warning of the dreadful storm that is about to burst upon the earth below.

A sea like glass before the throne connects this scene to the Old Testament laver. The laver held cleansing water for the priests. It was located in the court of the tabernacle and later on, in Solomon's temple.

Four living creatures, or created beings, truly defy description (v. 8b-11). The best John could do was report that they were "full of eyes around and within." We will not try to improvise words that escaped the apostle as he observed these remarkable beings. We may not know exactly what they looked like, but we do know what their job description was: they were a quartet which proclaimed that holy anthem,

"Holy, holy, holy,

Lord God Almighty,

Who was and is and is to come!" (Revelation 4:8)

The elders respond to their song with a declaration that reveals the ultimate purpose of man, to proclaim His worth and follow His will (v. 11).

Heaven is going to blow our minds. Today our imagination is overwhelmed by descriptions of heaven even with the limited details we are given. However, what we see vaguely now in our imaginations will soon be live—the full revelation of His glory in living color.

Three points of application are found in this chapter. First, the trumpet call is also for us today, so if you hear His call, do not harden your heart. Secondly, God is a rewarder of those who pursue Him with an honest heart. There is a great falling away predicted, which caused Jesus to wonder, "Nevertheless, when the Son of Man comes, will he find faith on the earth?" (Luke 18:8b). What a heartbreaking question! Finally, the door to heaven is still open, and now is the time of salvation.

Do not let heaven's door close in your life. You do not want to be left outside of His grace!

SICKNESS OF THE SOUL

Hatred is consuming our nation just as anxiety and depression have gripped this land. Anxiety disorders are the most common mental illness in the United States, affecting 40 million adults age 18 and older.[2]

Twenty times in the book of Revelation a loud voice asks the same question many are asking today, "Who is worthy?" Indeed, who has the character and credentials to assume the position of the Messiah? All humans are disqualified according to Romans 3:23, "All have sinned and come short of the glory of God."

John despairs but the elders encourage him not to weep because there is One who is worthy (5:4-5). The Lion of the tribe of Judah was willing to become a lamb and serve sacrificially as the ultimate sin offering.

Therefore, today the church can boldly proclaim to a sin-soaked world, "Do not weep, Christ has prevailed where mankind failed." John sees Christ appearing as a lamb who had been slain (vv. 6-7). The result of the first coming of Jesus on earth was the atoning sacrifice of the spotless Lamb of God (Hebrews 9:11-12). Yes, our once-wounded Redeemer stands as a permanent testament to God's determination to redeem mankind.

It has been noted that in heaven, the only thing mankind will contribute will be the scars on the Savior. In fact, the only thing we bring to salvation is the sin that made it necessary.

A NEW SONG

The proper response to the magnificence of Jesus is exhibited when the elders and four creatures around the throne fall before the Lord in an attitude of praise as they sing a new song.

And they sang a new song, saying:

"You are worthy to take the scroll,

And to open its seals;

For You were slain,

And have redeemed us to God by Your blood

Out of every tribe and tongue and people and nation." (Revelation 5:9)

Notice, it is a song for every tribe, tongue, people, and nation which tells us that despite failings of the church, ultimately the great commission will be fulfilled. This song is not exclusive to any race, gender, or social status. All who have been rescued from death row by the sacrifice of Jesus will·be welcome to join in. Only Christ the Lamb of God can heal man's sin-sick condition and make us clean—as white as snow.

10

PREVIEW OF COMING ATTRACTIONS

Revelation 6

"I think it rather pathetic that so many people are looking forward to heaven to prove their doctrinal position correct." – Chuck Smith[1]

Now I saw when the Lamb opened one of the seals; and I heard one of the four living creatures saying with a voice like thunder, "Come and see." And I looked, and behold, a white horse. He who sat on it had a bow; and a crown was given to him, and he went out conquering and to conquer. When He opened the second seal, I heard the second living creature saying, "Come and see." (Revelation 6:1–3)

"Come and see" is the invitation as the seven seals are removed one by one from the scroll. The breaking of the seals initiates a preview of the coming seven-year tribulation period (Revelation 6–19:4).

The first broken seal reveals a white horse and its rider. The rider of the white horse is the first of four horsemen that are loosed on the earth by the breaking of the first four seals. Some believe the first rider is Christ. However, it is most likely the Antichrist, and his identity is revealed by two key details.

DIFFERENT CROWN, DIFFERENT WEAPON

First, we find different crowns. The Greek word for the crown given to this rider is *stephanos*, implying one given permission to rule. Man's rebellion has given Satan permission to reign. However God has limited his reign, as the book of Job illustrates. The Antichrist will have limited power, but he is capable of wreaking havoc on earth.

Satan's crown is different from the crown of Christ (Revelation 14:14), which is a diadem, implying supreme victory. The diadem is for a true sovereign king, not one needing permission to rule.

We also find different weapons here. This rider is armed with a bow while Jesus is armed with a sword (Revelation 19:11–16). The bow indicates that this rider is a warrior and for a time he will prevail.

BROKEN SEALS

The second broken seal reveals a fiery red horse representing bloody warfare. During the seven-year tribulation period, all hope for peace will be taken from earth (vv. 5-6).

The third broken seal reveals a black horse whose rider had a pair of scales in his hand representing scarcity and famine. The extent of the famine during the tribulation period can be seen in the latter part of verse 6, "A quart of wheat for a denarius, and three quarts of barley for a denarius." The ratio represents working a full day for bare subsistence. This speaks of worldwide hunger on a scale beyond what we can currently imagine.

FAMINE

Throughout history, famine has ravaged the human race often as a result of warfare or natural disasters. Death by starvation is dreadful and painful. The young and the elderly are often hit first and hardest during a famine. During the recent famine in North Korea, the childhood mortality rate rose to 93 out of 1000 children, and over a four-year span, an estimated 2.5–3 million people perished due to malnutrition and starvation. This situation was the result of tyrannical incompetence. By comparison, World War I was the root cause of 5 million deaths between 1917 and 1921.

Much like the Soviet Famine of 1932 to 1933, which took 10 million lives, the Great Chinese Famine of the 1950s was caused by Communist leaders attempting to force change upon an unwilling population. As part of the so-called Great Leap Forward, 43 million Chinese perished.[2]

As dreadful as these and other famines were, the black horse of the fourth broken seal will usher in unprecedented worldwide deprivation and death. And yet, as has always been the case, aristocratic warlords and rulers will have no lack (v. 6b). This hypocrisy, captured in Marie Antoinette's famous statement, "Let them eat cake," is symbolic of those who live in luxury and excess while the famine-stricken masses languish away.

The fifth of seven broken seals (vv. 9–11) reveals another scene: the cry of the martyrs. This vision is symbolic of those believers who will come to Christ after the rapture of the church, those who will give their very lives for their faith in Christ.

They are envisioned as being under the altar, representing the brazen altar in the court of the Old Testament temple. Their place under the altar speaks of Christ's sacrifice and divine covering for these saints.

Still they cry out for revenge against their prosecutors, asking "How long, Lord?" He who knows the end from the beginning comforts and encourages them to "wait a while longer" (v. 11b). Their waiting will not be in vain.

But let justice run down like water,

And righteousness like a mighty stream. (Amos 5:24)

WORK WHILE THERE IS STILL LIGHT

With the church evacuated, Satan's efforts become frantically escalated (Revelation 12:12) and the efforts of the Holy Spirit are now redirected. We are reminded that today is the time to upgrade our efforts for the Kingdom.

For the mystery of lawlessness is already at work; only He who now restrains will do so until He is taken out of the way. (2 Thessalonians 2:7)

At the current time, the restrainer holds back the forces of lawlessness, preventing them from having full reign on earth. Only the Holy Spirit has the influence to hold back evil and His chosen vessels for expression are found in His power to convict through the church.

Of course, the Holy Spirit is omnipresent, but after the church is removed between chapters three and four, He will have voluntarily reduced His restraining activities. Once this unique ministry is gone, lawlessness and sin will reach unimaginable levels of manifestation. This is very bad news for the inhabitants of earth.

You do not want to be here for Satan's coming out party and you do not have to be. If you are the least bit unsure of your spiritual condition, I urge you to consider the promise of Jesus to forgive sinners. Please take time right now to consider John 3:16 and accept forgiveness. This will be the best and most important decision you could ever make.

"For God so loved the world that He gave His only begotten Son, that whoever believes in Him should not perish but have everlasting life." (John 3:16)

God loves justice and hates injustice, and He commands His people to uphold justice. Further, He wants us to actively work for justice—especially for the vulnerable.

"Learn to do right; seek justice. Defend the oppressed. Take up the cause of the fatherless; plead the case of the widow." (Isaiah 1:17)

In following this and many similar commands from the Bible, the church is expected to stand up for what is right even when others don't. In this broken world, our best efforts will still fall short. But fear not. Inevitably, Jesus will establish justice for everyone on earth, and that will include those waiting beneath the altar.

Beloved, do not avenge yourselves, but rather give place to wrath; for it is written, "Vengeance is Mine, I will repay," says the Lord. (Romans 12:19)

HEADLINES IN HEAVEN

We have become accustomed to the intrusion of "Breaking News" into our lives. At one time, before the advent of the 24/7 cable news cycle, true breaking news was significant and noteworthy. Today, that is not the case. It seems that every hour brings some sort of news alert. Thus, what makes the news on earth has been diluted by the advent of multiple round the clock news platforms.

So let us ask the question, "What makes news in heaven?" Good question, and an important one. Let us be clear, events on earth are of great interest in heaven. For example, angels are intrigued by the process of salvation of fallen mankind. Peter indicates in his first letter that salvation is so wonderful that angels are anxiously watching these events unfold (1:12).

Unfortunately, most of the news that hits the headlines in heaven is scandalous in nature. Pure and holy inhabitants of heaven are astonished by the behavior of mere man. How can the creation be so determined to insult their Creator? Why has the hoax of evolution captured the hearts and minds of the best and brightest of the modern world? What would possess millions of women to sacrifice their children on the altar of sexual expediency? It would seem that the depravity of fallen man is a mystery to the divine counsel of super beings that populate the heavens and surround the throne.

SECOND COMING FONT

In journalism circles, *second coming type* is legendarily the largest headline font a newspaper would ever print. The old saying was purported to go something like, "Anything less than the second coming of Christ, stay below this size." In the past century, these six events have qualified for this level of front-page space in the United States:

- Pearl Harbor
- Atomic Bomb Dropped
- World War II Ends
- JFK Killed
- Man on the Moon
- 9/11

WHAT GETS THE ATTENTION OF HEAVEN

We do know that God has an appreciative audience for His magnificent works of creation and salvation.

When the morning stars sang together,

And all the sons of God shouted for joy? (Job 38:7)

"I say to you that likewise there will be more joy in heaven over one sinner who repents than over ninety-nine just persons who need no repentance." (Luke 15:7)

Not only do the angels and elders take interest in the affairs of man, but those who have relocated to heaven are also keenly aware of events on earth.

When He opened the fifth seal, I saw under the altar the souls of those who had been slain for the word of God and for the testimony which they held. And they cried with a loud voice, saying, "How long, O Lord, holy and true, until You judge and avenge our blood on those who dwell on the earth?" Then a white robe was given to each of them; and it was said to them that they should rest a little while longer, until both the number of their fellow servants and

their brethren, who would be killed as they were, was completed.
(Revelation 6:9 – 11)

From these three verses, we can make these observations about saints in heaven. They are:

- Vocal and loud
- Passionate and emotional
- Aware of each other, God, and events on earth
- Capable of asking God to intervene
- Concerned about injustice
- Conscious of their own murder
- Impatient for God's intervention
- Eager to see their martyrdom avenged

PERSECUTION OF THE SAINTS: OUTRAGEOUS

According to various mission organizations, thousands of Christians are killed for their faith each year. Obviously, evil regimes do not publish statistics on these atrocities. But the true number of martyrs is outrageous news in heaven and does not go unnoticed.

For perspective, Open Doors USA has these observations about the most dangerous places on earth to have faith in Jesus Christ.[3]

1. North Korea–Christians are considered hostile elements to be eradicated.
2. Afghanistan—Christianity is not permitted to exist.
3. Somalia–Christians are high-value targets.
4. Libya—Believers face abuse and deadly violence.
5. Pakistan—Christians live with the constant threat of mob attacks.

6. Sudan—Converts to Christianity are targeted for persecution.
7. Eritrea (Near Ethiopia and Sudan)—Christians are imprisoned and killed.
8. Yemen—The church is especially vulnerable in civil war and famine.
9. Iran—It is illegal to convert and illegal to preach.
10. India—Christians are subjected to unprecedented violence.

MOST BANNED BOOK?

In 1989, Salman Rushdie's *The Satanic Verses* was banned or burned in 11 different countries and resulted in a fatwa being issued against the author when the Iranian Ayatollah Khomeni ordered Muslims to kill him.

This incident pales in comparison to over 50 nations where the Bible is either illegal or severely suppressed. Bible smugglers have been arrested and jailed for decades in closed countries, and we can be sure that the residents of heaven take note and are not pleased.

Remember our reviews of chapters 2 and 3 tell us that Jesus pays attention to the details of His church. Since nothing escapes Him about the beloved Bride, we can be certain those who persecute her will face serious consequences eventually.

Like the group of saints gathered under the altar, many throughout the bloodstained pages of history have asked, "How long, Lord?" with good reason. Evil people so often seem to triumph while good men suffer at their hands. Justice is absolutely a primary biblical concern.

One example is Dietrich Bonhoeffer, heralded as a hero of the Christian church for his bravery during World War II. Many in the German church cooperated with the Nazis, but Bonhoeffer actively resisted and paid dearly for his decision.

As the Allies closed in on Berlin in April of 1945, he had been imprisoned for cooperating in plots to assassinate the Fuhrer. As Allied occupation became inevitable, Hitler took his own life, but not before giving orders for Bonhoeffer to be executed. We can be certain Dietrich is among those in heaven at this very moment awaiting the Lord's vengeance upon evil persons.

HOW TO MAKE HEADLINES IN HEAVEN

Here is a good question to ask: Who impressed Jesus?

Remember who was chosen to walk with Him. It wasn't Pharisees, generals, or political leaders. No, after a night of prayer, Jesus picked fishermen, a rebel, and a tax-collector. We speculate that Judas was the most "respectable" apostle, and we know how that turned out.

"Whoever humbles himself as this child, he is the greatest in the kingdom of heaven." (Matthew 18:4).

Here are some quick questions worthy of consideration.

- What is the headline over your life?
- What does your story say?
- Where is your story making news?
- What would your obituary say?

These are good issues for all to consider. Think especially about where your story is getting attention. Would it be on the business page, the sports page, or heaven's front page?

One way to answer these legacy questions is to write your obituary as it would stand today. Are you pleased with it? If there are areas you would like to edit and improve on, now is the time. The deadline for your final edition is near.

CHAOS IN THE COSMOS

The breaking of the sixth seal (vv. 12–17) reveals a disruption of our solar system prophesied by Jesus (Luke 21:25–16). How dreadful! In desperation, people will attempt to hide from Him who sits on the throne. They can run, but they cannot hide from the Living God.

This illuminates an interesting point: even when the reality of God is inescapable, people run from Him, not to Him.

In the first four seals, the living creatures invited John to "come and see" the horrific events that are soon to take place. John is also given an audience to observe firsthand what Christ has delivered His people from: the destructive agenda of the devil. Here we find a world impoverished not only spiritually but also physically during the great tribulation period. Satan also seeks to rob mankind of hope by blinding humans to the glorious grace of total forgiveness.

Remember, as Jonathan Edwards observed, grace is total; therefore, we too should follow the invitation to come and see, but better yet, "taste and see" (Psalm 34:8).

MANKIND: BETTER EVERY DAY IN EVERY WAY?

In the bloodstained pages of history, humans have endured the manmade horrors of genocide, world wars, gulags, concentration camps, and killing fields. Anyone who imagines the human race transcending into a superior species needs a reality check. They should first confront the fact that the 20th century was the bloodiest ever, in spite of all our advancements.

> "The 20th century was the most murderous in recorded history. The total number of deaths caused by or associated with its wars has been estimated at 187m, the equivalent of more than 10% of the world's population in 1913. Taken as having begun in 1914, it was a century of almost unbroken war, with few and brief periods without organised armed conflict somewhere." – Eric Hobsbawm[4]

- Some 75 million people died in World War II, including about 20 million military personnel and 40 million civilians, many of whom died because of deliberate genocide, massacres, mass-bombings, disease, and starvation.[5]
- Communism was the leading ideological cause of death between 1900 and 2000. Ninety-four million perished in China, the Soviet Union, North Korea, Afghanistan, and Eastern Europe.[6]

Nature has also provided its own catalog of terror through the ages as earthquakes, tsunamis, hurricanes, and droughts have decimated populations.

None of these traumas compare with what will confront mankind when the pent-up judgments of God are finally unleashed. This is the storm of storms. Only those on their knees will be able to stand.

DEATH HAS BEEN DEFEATED

"O Death, where is your sting? O Hades, where is your victory?" (1 Corinthians 15:55)

Then Death and Hades were cast into the lake of fire. This is the second death. (Revelation 20:14)

"The Bible repeatedly tells us that someday Christ will return— not in weakness, the way He came the first time, but with power and glory, and with great authority" – Billy Graham[7]

Jesus said, "For then shall be great tribulation, such as was not since the beginning of the world to this time, no, nor ever shall be. And except those days should be shortened, there should no flesh be saved: but for the elect's sake those days shall be shortened" (Matthew 24:21–22 KJV).

UNIMAGINABLE HORRORS OF THE COMING TRIBULATION

Here is a partial list of what an unrepentant humanity will face.

- Demonic forces will be allowed to take on grotesque shapes and forms and present themselves to torment and destroy sinful people.
- Disease and plagues will be mutated into dark forms and there will be no cure.
- Mankind will find out what happens when humans are free to act without restraint.

- The earth will become a God-forsaken, hellish place to live and to die upon.
- Grievous sores will cover men, much like running boils or cancers.
- The sea will be turned into blood, as that of a dead man, and everything will die.
- All fresh water, streams, rivers, and fountains of waters will become blood.
- The sun will become so hot it will scorch men with fire to burn them alive.
- Darkness will cover the land and cause men to gnaw their tongues in distress, implying that this darkness must cause some form of pain.
- Rivers will be dried up to allow the gathering of kings and men to Armageddon for man's last stand against God Almighty.
- Earthquakes will occur.
- Hailstones of 100-pound weight will fall from the sky.
- Every mountain will fall down flat, and islands will sink.

STORMS ON THE HORIZON

Hurricane trackers watch storms form off the coast of Africa, following them every step of the way across the Atlantic. Many lives are saved because modern technology allows advance warning and evacuation.

In earlier times, coastal residents may have recognized the onset of a storm, but there was no accurate means to predict its path or power. Therefore, many perished. Today, sophisticated models and mass media make it possible to avoid this fate. Yet when Hurricane Katrina approached New Orleans with class five ferocity, Bourbon Street bars remained open even when a direct hit became inevitable. This all took place in a city that is built below sea level. Nearly two thousand people perished from Katrina and the ensuing floods.

This tragic story parallels much of the reaction to warnings about the coming storm of the Tribulation and the second coming of Jesus.

The church's warnings about the apocalypse are not happening in secret. Despite the shortcomings of the church detailed in Chapters 1–3, and the attending apathy towards the great commission in many churches, the gospel message is going out as never before. Fifteen hundred radio stations in America alone are dedicated to Christian programming. Television, the internet, and publishing are all packed with Christian content.

There is a storm coming. Whether by natural death or the coming tribulation—all of mankind will face a storm. When the winds are already hitting 150 MPH, that's not a good time to put up hurricane shutters.

Deathbed conversions are dangerous and difficult to time.

The time to prepare is now. Don't be left behind.

11

REMNANT OF MERCY

Revelation 7

"Imagine for a moment what it will be like when the winds stop and it becomes dead calm. There will be no breeze, no movement of leaves in the trees, and no movement of the clouds, and the ocean waters will become completely calm. It will be as if the Lord has turned off the engine of the earth. But make no mistake, this is the eye of the storm and a temporary interlude to God's continuing judgement." – Jeff Lasseigne[1]

After these things I saw four angels standing at the four corners of the earth, holding the four winds of the earth, that the wind should not blow on the earth, on the sea, or on any tree. Then I saw another angel ascending from the east, having the seal of the living God. And he cried with a loud voice to the four angels to whom it was granted to harm the earth and the sea, saying, "Do not harm the earth, the sea, or the trees till we have sealed the servants of our God on their foreheads." (Revelation 7:1–3)

THE RESTRAINED & THE REMNANT

The planet earth is a stage. A drama of cosmic proportions is being played out for all of creation to watch, causing us to marvel at the things which take place. Enter five angels, four to hold back the winds and one bearing a seal of God. He will use the seal to mark certain people who are chosen as special servants to God. They will be protected and preserved in the face of divine wrath being unleashed on the earth.

The seal of eastern kings was stamped in a signet ring and worn as a sign of authority. This remnant is clearly Jewish (Revelation 7:5–8), representing the twelve tribes of Israel, chosen to evangelize a terrified world. This does not mean that only those of Jewish heritage come to salvation during the tribulation period, but rather these have been selected for His specific purposes.

Note that the tribe of Dan is omitted from this list due to their relentless pursuit of idolatry (Leviticus 24:11; Judges 18; 1 Kings 12:28–30). Idolatry, in this context, is the worship of the Antichrist—an accepted worldwide practice during this tribulation period. The tribe of Dan is replaced by the tribe of Manasseh, who was one of Joseph's sons.

And so the divine dominoes are lined up for God to continue the plan that began before the foundation of the world.

We are treading on holy ground when we pretend to fully understand the mechanics of God's ways. But in hindsight we can clearly observe many implications and results of His actions. Chief among the surprises was His absurd choice for a chosen people, the Jews.

"What is the Jew?...What kind of unique creature is this whom all the rulers of all the nations of the world have disgraced and crushed and expelled and destroyed; persecuted, burned and drowned, and who, despite their anger and their fury, continues to live and to flourish. What is this Jew whom they have never succeeded in enticing with all the enticements in the world, whose oppressors and persecutors only suggested that he deny (and disown) his religion and cast aside the faithfulness of his ancestors?!

The Jew – is the symbol of eternity. . .He is the one who for so long had guarded the prophetic message and transmitted it to all mankind. A people such as this can never disappear.

The Jew is eternal. He is the embodiment of eternity."– Leo Tolstoy[2]

WHY CHOOSE THE JEWS?

Legendarily, it is said that Queen Victoria asked British Prime Minister Benjamin Disraeli for the greatest evidence of the existence of God. To which he is said to have replied, "The Jews your Majesty, the Jews."

Why did God choose the Jews? Not because they were clever but because they were not.

"The LORD did not set His love on you nor choose you because you were more in number than any other people, for you were the least of all peoples." (Deuteronomy 7:7)

When a sculptor chooses a stone to become his masterpiece, he does not pick soft marble.

What is the best-known work of stone art in America? Mount Rushmore no doubt, which is difficult to reach and was a huge challenge to complete. This impressive site remains a lasting testament to the artist. So it is with Israel. The Jews were unlikely candidates to become a canvas for the King. It certainly was not because they were humble or easy to deal with. Quite the opposite was true.

"Therefore understand that the LORD your God is not giving you this good land to possess because of your righteousness, for you are a stiff-necked people." (Deuteronomy 9:6)

PHARAOH, HAMAN, HEROD, AND HITLER

It is controversial to identify which Pharaoh was involved in the Exodus, but whichever Pharaoh it was, there's no doubt he hated the Jews.

Why are the Jews historically and consistently hated? As folksinger Tom Lehrer wrote, "Oh the Protestants hate the Catholics, and the Catholics hate the Protestants, and the Hindus hate the Moslems, and everybody hates the Jews."[3]

In the wonderful story from the book of Esther, Haman is the archenemy of the Jews. He plots their total destruction. Irony is layered upon irony as the Jews are marvelously rescued by the invisible hand of God. Invisible because God is never mentioned in the pages of this book, though His fingerprints are never absent from a single scene.

Despite God's repeated rescues of this people, their persecution has continued in the millennia since Bible times. Jews have been expelled from over eighty countries, persecuted beyond measure, and nearly annihilated by the Nazis. And yet they have defied every onslaught and survived as God's chosen people.

In a classic scene from the Academy Award winning film, *Fiddler on The Roof*, Tevye, the star and Jewish immigrant, wonders, "I know, I know, we are Your chosen people. But, once in a while, can't You choose someone else?"[4] This is a reasonable request given that God's favor also puts an illuminating spotlight of human hatred on the Jews.

Antisemitism has methodically stained the pages of history ever since ancient days in Egypt, during the time of Moses. No people group has suffered so severely yet prospered so astonishingly as the Jews. Herod and his infamous historical colleagues are in fact merely puppets in this long running drama. It is Satan himself who has long been pulling the strings of humanity, resulting in these unrelenting, murderous assaults on the Jewish people. Remember, the Adversary is not all-knowing, so he fights with a shotgun instead of a sharpshooter. He does not know exactly how or when God will execute His promised rescue through the Jews. So he has sought to stomp them out categorically.

Author and researcher Lisa Katz provides some helpful insights on Jewish accomplishments.[5] With an estimated 7.4 billion people on earth, Jews comprise a mere 0.2 percent of the human population. This makes the following list of accomplishments by Jews particularly impressive.

Between 1901 and 2015, 194 Nobel prizes have been awarded to Jews, accounting for 22 percent of all Nobel prizes awarded. This is more than 100 times what they should win based strictly on random chance. In fact, Jews have won more Nobel prizes than any other ethnicity, even though they make up a minute portion of the earth's population.

JEWISH STARS OF SCIENCE, BUSINESS, AND LITERATURE

Albert Einstein, perhaps the most famous scientist of the 20th century, proposed a groundbreaking theory of relativity, including his famous equation $e=mc^2$.

Dr. Jonas Salk created the first polio vaccine.

Dr. Albert Sabin developed the first oral polio vaccine

Hart, Schaffner, Marx, Kuppenheimer, and Levi Strauss became household names in men's clothing.

Isadore & Nathan Straus ("Abraham & Straus") became sole owners of Macy's, the world's largest department store, in 1896.

Armand Hammer (Arm & Hammer) was a physician and businessman who originated the largest trade between the U.S. and Russia.

Louis Santanel was the financier who provided the funds for Columbus' voyage.

Jews account for 53 percent of the recipients of the Pulitzer Prize for General Non-Fiction and 14 percent of recipients for fiction.

"If the statistics are right, the Jews constitute but one quarter of one percent of the human race. It suggests a nebulous puff of stardust lost in the blaze of the Milky Way. Properly, the Jew ought hardly to be heard of, but he is heard of, has always been heard of. He is as prominent on the planet as any other people, and his importance is extravagantly out of proportion to the smallness of his bulk. His contributions to the world's list of great names in literature, science, art, music, finance, medicine, and abstruse learning are also way out of proportion to the weakness of his numbers. He has made a marvelous fight in the world, in all the ages; and has done it with his hands tied behind him. The Egyptian, the Babylonian, and the Persian rose, filled the planet with sound and splendor, then faded to dream-stuff and passed away; the Greek and the Roman followed, and made a vast noise, and they are gone; other peoples have sprung up and held their torch high for a time, but it burned out, and they sit in twilight now, or have vanished. All things are mortal but the Jew; all other forces pass, but he remains. What is the secret of his immortality?" - Mark Twain[6]

READ LAMENTATIONS AND WEEP

Great position and privilege come with tremendous responsibility. Time and again, the Jewish nation was clearly warned of dire penalties that would occur if they failed to observe Jehovah as the one true God. Sieges, suffering, and exile are among the testimonies to their historic failures. We should read and weep of the catalog of consequences they endured. And weep is exactly what Jesus did over their fate.

Now as He drew near, He saw the city and wept over it, saying, "If you had known, even you, especially in this your day, the things that make for your peace! But now they are hidden from your eyes." (Luke 19:41–42)

During its long history, Jerusalem has been attacked 52 times, captured and recaptured 44 times, besieged 23 times, and destroyed twice.[7]

THE CLOCK STARTS TICKING: MAY 14, 1948

Time and again, the Old Testament records that God was faithful to establish a nation through Abraham just as He would prove dependable in maintaining the throne of David.

The Jews suffered a dispersion of nearly 2,000 years. The Romans forbade a Jew to set foot in Jerusalem and changed the name of the city to stamp out Judaism, even forbidding the presence of Jewish Scripture.

Every demonic and human device has been unleashed against them over the years, and still the Jews were again established in Israel in 1948. Today, the capitals of the world are puzzled by Israel's very existence. No larger than the nation of Paraguay, Israel still consistently dominates world headlines regularly. Everyone knows the name *Jerusalem*, while no one remembers the Romans' failed rebrand of *Aelia Capitolina*.

THE REJOICING

One of many astonishing scenes now unfolds to John when he sees a great multitude standing in white with palm branches before the throne of God (vv. 9–17). This breathtaking display of great joy is a glorious portrait of true worship, an expression that crosses all racial, geographic, linguistic, and cultural lines.

Just think of it: everyone in true unity, with one heart and one mind, all in adoration of the Lamb.

The life that orbits around the one true God is dramatically in contrast to the world John sees under the Antichrist. We see joy versus dread, peace as opposed to terror, and love in contrast to tyranny.

Torment and tears cease (v. 17). Weeping will be transformed to fountains of living water. Haunting turns to healing when broken hearts are mended.

This will be a glorious moment, but you need not wait if you are suffering from great distress. Jesus can heal the broken pieces of your heart today. Yes, the process will be perfectly accomplished on that great day, but even now the Lord can be your shepherd. He will lead you by still waters and cause you to lie down in green grass (Psalm 23).

God has a remnant in every generation. His remnant is not a group of perfect people who never fail, but of saints who enjoy their standing only because they hope in His mercy.

12

DELAYED JUDGMENT RELEASED

Revelation 8

"In a time of global pandemics, people are understandably frightened...What the Bible teaches is most important in such times is that we individually, personally and humbly seek God's forgiveness and mercy, and get ourselves spiritually ready for the return of Jesus Christ by reading and obeying the Bible, which is the holy Word of God." – Joel Rosenberg[1]

When He opened the seventh seal, there was silence in heaven for about half an hour. (Revelation 8:1)

WHEN GOD HITS THE BRAKES

Thirty minutes of silence in heaven. Think of it: the seraphim's anthem, "Holy, holy, holy," ceases— perhaps for the first and only time in eternity.

Furthermore:

- There were no trumpets, thunder, or lightning around the throne (Revelation 4:5).
- A choir of countless angels grew silent (Revelation 5:11–12).
- The doors and thresholds of the temple stopped shaking in response (Isaiah 6:4).
- The 24 elders around the throne of God set their harps aside temporarily (Revelation 5:8).
- The wings of the cherubim no longer made the sound of water crashing on the shore (Ezekiel 1:24).

More heavenly sounds that aren't mentioned also ceased during this remarkable time of silence. We know this because the apostle Paul heard "inexpressible things" (2 Corinthians 12:3–4) in heaven that he was not permitted to talk about.

This is a moment so significant that one might say, "God hit the brakes, hard." There are other significant moments throughout history when God seems to have brought everything to a standstill.

2020 VISION

The year 2020 seemed to be a year of promise, a time of fresh starts. 2020 was a new year, a different decade, and a cool number that brought up images of crisp vision and a clear view of a hopeful future. Like many New Year's resolutions, those bright plans lasted barely past Valentine's Day. As Mike Tyson famously said, "Everyone has a plan until they get punched in the mouth."[2] And wow, did planet earth get punched in the mouth in 2020.

Quarantine became the norm and toilet paper a gold standard. Strange days indeed.

THE ULTIMATE QUARANTINE

When the world does not make sense, it is wise to look to the One who does. Periodically throughout history as recorded in the Bible, the Lord hits the brakes in a very serious way. Mankind better have their spiritual seat belts on whenever that happens.

For example, imagine a time so evil that God regretted He had even created man and woman. It happened in the time of Noah.

Then the LORD saw that the wickedness of man was great in the earth, and that every intent of the thoughts of his heart was only evil continually. And the LORD was sorry that He had made man on the earth, and He was grieved in His heart. So the LORD said, "I will destroy man whom I have created from the face of the earth, both man and beast, creeping thing and birds of the air, for I am sorry that I have made them." (Genesis 6:5–7)

Poorly done, mankind. Only a few chapters after God's declaration that all of His creation was "very good" (Genesis 1:31), humans had managed to exhaust the last nerve of the most patient Person ever.

BUT NOAH FOUND GRACE

Let us never underestimate the grace of God.

Noah and his family were identified to receive the unmerited favor of the Lord (Genesis 6:8). So Noah had a choice: build a giant ship on his front lawn or learn to tread water for a very long time. He chose the former, resulting in one of the best-known stories of all time.

Still, let's not lose the storyline here and its relevance to the corona lockdown that occurred in 2020. Noah and his family were put in quarantine by God Himself. The Bible says God shut the door of the ark (Genesis 7:16).

Note that until Jesus arrived on the scene and was touching all sorts of people, there are only a few examples of God's literal hand intruding on earth, such as forming man from dust (Genesis 2:7), burying Moses (Deuteronomy 34:5–6), and here, closing the ark. Remember, Noah and company did not have the benefit of foresight; they were not informed how long their journey would be, when or where they might land, and why they had two of every animal in the world on board. But they would soon find out.

LEVITICUS LOCKDOWN

Leprosy is an ugly disease. You may think it is ancient and eradicated, but you would be wrong.

Even now, seven million people worldwide are infected by leprosy, though a cure has existed for decades. Six hundred new cases are diagnosed each day worldwide.

In Old and New Testament times, there was no human cure for leprosy. In Leviticus 13, we find detailed directions for the effective social quarantine of lepers. Thus, we find that once again, God takes drastic action to protect His people.

STAY INSIDE

When Moses took his rightful place at the head of the Hebrew nation temporarily residing in Egypt, we find another prime example of a God-ordained lock in. This quarantine was only for one night, but it was not optional if you wanted to avoid the angel of death.

And you shall take a bunch of hyssop, dip it in the blood that is in the basin, and strike the lintel and the two doorposts with the blood that is in the basin. And none of you shall go out of the door of his house until morning. For the LORD will pass through to strike the Egyptians; and when He sees the blood on the lintel and on the two doorposts, the LORD will pass over the door and not allow the destroyer to come into your houses to strike you. (Exodus 12:22–23)

This great Passover was to be a permanent memorial for the people of Jehovah to remember the great deliverance from death provided by their God.

DO WE DESERVE THIS?

People will ponder the genesis of this Covid-19 plague from medical, geo-political, and spiritual vantage points. Was the virus preventable? Did a malicious foreign state intentionally unleash hell on humanity? Is this a plague sent as punishment by God?

The first two questions are left for history to sort out, so we address the third. First, let's consider the question, "Does God send plagues to afflict man?"

Some pestilence is simply the result of a broken creation, such as the dust storms of the 1930s in middle America. Others are a function of God allowing His protection to be removed. But in many biblical cases, plagues were specifically sent to chastise either pagan nations or His people Israel.

Let there be no doubt that God is intensely aware of the growing insults hurled at Him by man. Evolution insists that He did not make us. Sexual identity advocates reject that man is made male and female. Abortion activists consider it health care to kill His innocent heritage in the womb.

Despite these and other travesties, God's cup of wrath is not overflowing—yet. That day will come, and you definitely want to miss that party.

But this is not that.

VACATION WITH A PURPOSE

Far from being a curse, we find that a quarantine can be a great blessing if properly approached and experienced. Beyond the obvious deliverance from destruction, this time can also be seen as an opportunity to rest, reset, and revive. Soon enough, in God's grace we will be allowed to go out and play again in the fields of the Lord.

PESTILENCE AND PLAGUES

Joel Rosenburg asks, "What are God's sovereign purposes for using such terrible diseases?" Rosenberg also offers the following answers:

- Executing divine judgment on an individual, a nation, or many nations for chronic, unrepentant sin.
- Warning other individuals and nations that they, too, could face divine judgment for chronic, unrepentant sin.
- Shaking an individual, nation, or many nations so that they will wake up from spiritual slumber or rebellion, repent of their sins, and turn in faith to a holy, personal, Biblical, healthy relationship with God.[3]

So it seems that pestilence and plagues are one way God puts humanity on pause to gain our attention. He wants to remind us of our frailty and mortality, not to mention mankind's penchant both for neglecting and provoking God.

Our study of the book of Revelation reveals the climax of devastating plagues on planet earth. Billions will perish under the scourges that John foresaw. We can also study epidemics of biblical magnitude that occurred from the Old Testament times to the New and throughout the pages of history.

A PLAGUE FOR PHARAOH

The book of Exodus records the best-known example in the Old Testament where God shook a nation to its core by inflicting horrible disease. Multiple movies have made a pale attempt to dramatize how terrible the events in Egypt really were. It is crucial to note that this contagion did not come without warning.

Then the LORD said to Moses, "Go in to Pharaoh and tell him, 'Thus says the LORD God of the Hebrews: "Let My people go, that they may serve Me. For if you refuse to let them go, and still hold them, behold, the hand of the LORD will be on your cattle in the field, on the horses, on the donkeys, on the camels, on the oxen, and on the sheep—a very severe pestilence." (Exodus 9:1–3)

The Exodus plagues remain the best-known examples, but this is far from the only time when the hand of God brought pestilence with a purpose. There were others aimed directly at Israel. But again, they were not without warning.

- Deuteronomy 28:15 says, "But it shall come to pass, if you do not obey the voice of the LORD your God, to observe carefully all His commandments and His statutes which I command you today, that all these curses will come upon you and overtake you."

- Deuteronomy 28:21 states, "The LORD will make the plague cling to you until He has consumed you from the land which you are going to possess."
- In Numbers 16:41–50, over 14,000 Israelites died of a divine plague, and it could have been worse if Moses and Aaron had not interceded.
- In 1 Samuel 5–6, God brings tumors on the Philistines. If you think there is no humor in heaven, you are missing the irony in these chapters. The Lord smote the Philistines with painful tumors and great confusion because of their impudence in placing the ark of God into the court of Dagon, their false god. The resulting plague was severe enough to cause the Philistines to evict the ark.
- In 2 Samuel 24:1, 70,000 men died when David angered the Lord. Once again, without the immediate intervention that occurred, wider deaths could have resulted. This event and the one mentioned above in Numbers show God's willingness to relent if people repent.

INFAMOUS PLAGUES IN HISTORY

- The most famous plague in non-biblical history is the Black Death of the 14th century, which was likely a disease now known as the bubonic plague. Estimates are that more than 20 million people—up to 50% of Europe's population—died in the outbreak.
- Killer flu: "Eighty years ago a sudden mutation in the virus that causes influenza initiated a worldwide epidemic that in only 18 months killed an estimated 25 to 40 million people around the world. Many consider

this to be the worst natural disaster in history" – Hillary Johnson[4]

BIOLOGICAL WARFARE

One of the first instances of biological warfare occurred in 1347 when the Mongols would catapult plague-infested corpses over the walls of a city they were laying siege to.

The Mongols may have been the first to use viral warfare, but they were not the last.

"Attempts to use biological warfare agents date back to antiquity. Scythian archers infected their arrows by dipping them in decomposing bodies or in blood mixed with manure as far back as 400 BC. Persian, Greek, and Roman literature from 300 BC quotes examples of dead animals used to contaminate wells and other sources of water. In the Battle of Eurymedon in 190 BC, Hannibal won a naval victory over King Eumenes II of Pergamon by firing earthen vessels full of venomous snakes into the enemy ships. ... During the French and Indian War in the 18th century AD, British forces under the direction of Sir Jeffrey Amherst gave blankets that had been used by smallpox victims to the Native Americans in a plan to spread the disease." – Edmond Hooker, MD, DrPH[5]

FAIR WARFARE?

The Geneva Protocol of 1925 was signed by 108 nations. This was the first multilateral agreement that extended prohibition of chemical agents to biological agents. In 1972, President Richard Nixon announced the end of the U.S. offensive biological weapons program and reaffirmed a no-first-use policy for chemical weapons. The key phrase here is "first use" because the fact is rogue regimes do not always play fair. Who are we going to trust to monitor and hold 180 plus countries accountable?

THE WORST WEAPON

Biological weapons have the potential to be the most destructive force in history. Atomic weapons have horrific local impact. They can also have regional and even global consequences, such as a nuclear winter. Viral weapons, however, have global possibilities, as various pandemics have already demonstrated. Anthrax, Ebola, yellow fever, and a hellish host of other diseases could be weaponized and they almost certainly exist now in laboratories around the world. Where atomic weapons demand a sophisticated level of research and development, biological weapons can be created with a comparatively lower level of science and cost.

Consider that in human history, every weapon devised and developed by mankind has eventually been unleashed. Could biological weapons contribute to the plagues of Revelation? That is not clear, but it is clear that the book of Revelation warns of terrible pestilence. These will come upon the earth as a judgment for the sins of mankind.

For example:

- A fourth of the earth is killed with sword, famine, and pestilence (Revelation 6:8).
- Two ambassadors from heaven usher in days of drought, rivers running with blood, and plagues (Revelation 11:6).

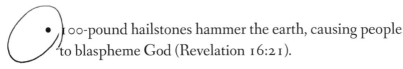
oo-pound hailstones hammer the earth, causing people to blaspheme God (Revelation 16:21).

POWER OF THE PLAGUE

The Bible clearly tells us that God uses plagues and pestilence to warn, wake, and judge. Many are fond of quoting 2 Chronicles 7:14 as a catalyst of hope to be found in national repentance:

"If My people who are called by My name will humble themselves, and pray and seek My face, and turn from their wicked ways, then I will hear from heaven, and will forgive their sin and heal their land." (2 Chronicles 7:14)

However, in expositional Bible study, context is a primary principle. So let's look back one verse.

"When I shut up heaven and there is no rain, or command the locusts to devour the land, or send pestilence among My people, if My people who are called by My name will humble themselves, and pray and seek My face, and turn from their wicked ways, then I will hear from heaven, and will forgive their sin and heal their land." (2 Chronicles 7:13-14)

Despite the cataclysmic events we find in the book of Revelation, God's grace remains. Shaking, waking, and judging are the threefold purposes of plagues and pestilences.

IGNORING GOD

Heaven holds its breath as the seventh seal is opened. The time of the Lord's vengeance has arrived (Romans 12:19).

When the Lord releases the brakes to let loose His judgment, there is no gradual acceleration. He goes from silence in heaven to all hell breaking loose on earth during the great tribulation period. Is this extreme action warranted?

Consider how the treatment of God has deteriorated in America. Prayer in schools was declared unconstitutional in America in 1962. Since then, the result has been a social disaster.

- Academic achievement has plummeted, including SAT scores.
- The out-of-wedlock birth rate has increased.
- Illegal drug use has grown dramatically.
- Juvenile crime has had a serious rise.

It seems almost quaint to read of the complaints of teachers in the 1950s—running in halls, chewing gum in class, and tardy students —when compared with the condition of public school classrooms since 1962. Today, profane language, violence, and drugs on campus top the list of destructive student behavior.

INSISTING ON MAN'S WAY

When Charles Darwin developed his theory of evolution, he could not have imagined the repercussions which would affect the coming generations. It should be no shock that if you teach children they are nothing but organized primates, they will eventually begin to act like animals. What else could be expected? Where should a moral code come from if there are no absolutes?

And so, we live in a culture that is reaping the whirlwind. Worse results may be ahead unless we nationally recognize evolution for what it is: a fraud. It is the greatest hoax of the past two centuries.

Apologizing to God for denying His status as Creator would be a good step. Just imagine standing by an artist's masterpiece and insisting the art created itself. That would seem a foolproof way to make the artist angry.

INSULTING GOD

Sixty million babies and counting. That is how many have died in this country through abortion since Roe v. Wade was handed down by our Supreme Court. Eventually America will discover what all pagan societies have found: there is a higher court. There is a truly Supreme Judge who rules over the affairs of man.

One Christian leader who shall go unnamed said this about abortion, "Well, in America, that ship has sailed." I can assure him and you that heaven does not view abortion as a closed case. Without repentance, judgment will come.

Further insults have resulted from the trendy fashion of denying that there are only two sexes in the human species. One social platform lets people "self-identify" as one of dozens of sexual types. This will not end well in our culture.

In a short amount of time, mainstream American thought has managed to deny, ignore, and insult the most basic truths of the book of Genesis.

- God is (He exists): In the beginning God... (Genesis 1:1).
- God created: He created the heavens and earth (Genesis 1:1).
- God ordered his creation with fixed human sexuality: Male and female He created them (Genesis 1:27).

Evolution, abortion, and transgenderism all violate God's basic revelation about Himself.

If the foundations are destroyed, What can the righteous do? (Psalm 11:3)

INEVITABLE JUDGMENT

The trumpet judgments in chapter 8 mark the start of the seven-year tribulation period prophesied in the book of Daniel (9:27). When the seals are broken on the scroll, the release of the trumpet judgments take place. The judgments occur during the first half of the great tribulation period, while the bowl judgments of Revelation 16 take place during the last half.

ALTAR OF INCENSE: PURIFY OR PUNISH

In the Jewish temple there was an altar of incense. It was one of three pieces of furniture found in the Holy Place. The altar of incense represented the prayers of the people with its smoke ascending upward. All of the various items in the tabernacle and the temple were models, or copies, of the true versions found in heaven (Hebrews 8:5). In verses 3 and 4, we find the heavenly version of the altar of incense, which contains the prayers of God's people.

Immediately after that (v. 5), we find an angel who fills his censer with hot coals from the altar and casts it upon the earth. Immediately there are noises, thunderings, lightnings, and an earthquake—an ominous and symbolic warning of things to come. Here we learn an important lesson: fire from the altar of God can either purify, as it did in Isaiah 6, or punish, as in the story of Aaron's two sons, Nadab and Abihu (Leviticus 6). These two presented strange fire before the Lord, and it destroyed them.

FIRST AND SECOND TRUMPETS, PLANTS, AND WATER

At this point, God's wrath is poised to be poured out, and the first trumpet sounds. An environmental disaster takes place when a third of the trees and grass are burned up.

The second trumpet brings about what John calls "a great mountain burning with fire," possibly a massive meteor. This mountain of fire is thrown into the sea. There is a threefold judgment here: a third of the sea becomes blood, a third of the sea creatures die, and a third of the ships are destroyed. In today's world, an estimated 50,000 merchant ships are on the sea at any one time. We can only imagine how devastating this disaster will be, and how it will affect global trade.

THIRD AND FOURTH TRUMPET

After the oceans are struck, the fresh waters are not spared either. The wrath of God now reaches inland, contaminating rivers and lakes (vv. 10-11). There appears to be a large molten object which falls from the heavens. The object probably disintegrates as it nears earth, dispersing into the various bodies of water. It will turn one-third of the freshwater springs and rivers on the earth into poison. The National Geographic Society lists one hundred principal rivers on earth, so we can only imagine the terrible effects of this disaster. We know that many people will die after this heavenly body falls to the earth. The name of this star is "Wormwood," representing a bitter aromatic plant that is synonymous with sorrow and great calamity.

The fourth trumpet brings on a judgment that is even more difficult to grasp when a third of the sun, moon, and stars are struck. The earth is darkened for a large part of the day. Jesus referred to this awful event in Luke 21:25–28. God will remove the very light He originally created. Of course, there will be very serious consequences as the seasons, human health, and crops will all be affected. In addition, due to the extra period of darkness, criminal activity will surge worldwide.

The silence has ended; the days of wrath are in full bloom on this rebel planet.

THE SEARCH FOR SODOM

Sodom and Gomorrah are the most infamous cities in history. The mere mention of these cities conjures up visions of decadent residents who collided with divine wrath. In view here is not *why* Sodom was judged (Genesis 16:13; Ezekiel 16:49) but rather *how*, in light of the coming Wormwood event, this destruction was accomplished.

Then the LORD rained upon Sodom and upon Gomorrah brimstone and fire from the LORD out of heaven; ... And he looked toward Sodom and Gomorrah, and toward all the land of the plain, and beheld, and, lo, the smoke of the country went up as the smoke of a furnace. (Genesis 19:24, 28 KJV)

For almost two decades, Dr. Steven Collins has been excavating a site in Jordan that he believes to be biblical Sodom. Tall el-Hammam lies west of Amman overlooking the Jordan River valley. On a clear day, Masada, Jerusalem, and Bethel are all visible to the east from the high ground of this ancient city site.

Fire and brimstone rained from heaven; Sodom was destroyed. It was also left desolate just as predicted in Jeremiah 50:40.

Dr. Collins and an international team of scholars have discovered evidence of what transpired when fire and brimstone rained from heaven. Sodom's destruction may have been a smaller-scale event pointing to the horrific day when Wormwood will strike the earth. Further, Sodom may not have been the only example of this type of devastation.[6]

On June 30, 1908, an asteroid exploded above Siberia, Russia. This has become known as the Tunguska event. The airburst flattened trees, killed reindeer, and did damage for hundreds of miles. The temperature of the fireball was so intense that silverware and tin utensils in the area were deformed by the heat. Eighty million trees were uprooted and blown down. Energy from this Siberian event was fifteen megatons, equal to about 1,000 atomic bombs of the same size as the one dropped on Hiroshima, Japan, at the end of World War II.[7]

Dr. Collins observes that both Sodom and Siberia can serve as signposts that the "finger of God" does indeed touch the land of man. It has before and when Wormwood strikes, it certainly will again.

13

THE DEFIANT ONES

Revelation 9

"With the fifth trumpet judgment, a shift of focus occurs-off of heaven and onto hell. All that heaven left undone in the previous devastations, Satan will now do. The time is coming when hell will visit the earth, bringing about a period of unprecedented terror."– Skip Heitzig[1]

Then the fifth angel sounded: And I saw a star fallen from heaven to the earth. To him was given the key to the bottomless pit.
(Revelation 9:1)

Since the Garden of Eden, man has refused to accept the straightforward consequences of defying God. This chapter is a further testament to the fact that rebellion is a dead-end street.

The fifth trumpet (v. 1) finds an army of locusts rising from the pit, having been set free by a leader who fell from heaven like a star. This fallen star is a person. Jesus declared, "I saw Satan fall like lightning from heaven" (Luke 10:18). The tense of the Greek verb for *fallen* here tells us that this star had already fallen from heaven.

A key to the bottomless pit is granted to this fallen star. He does not have complete authority here, or at any other time. Permission is granted to him according to God's will, for the purpose of releasing His wrath.

IT GETS PERSONAL

The judgment recorded here is not environmental like the ones that were heralded by the previous four trumpets. The fifth trumpet is focused on the inhabitants of the earth. The torment continues for five months (vv. 5-6), which is the normal life span of a locust. Their bites bring on symptoms like that of a painful scorpion sting. Scorpion stings can cause burning pain, facial swelling, and constricted breathing.

People will refuse to turn to God, seeking death instead. This decision is based on a misunderstanding of what happens to a person at death—it is no escape.

And as it is appointed for men to die once, but after this the judgment. (Heb 9:27)

There are different kinds of death because there are three different kinds of life, described by these Greek words:

- *Bios*: Biological life shared by humans, animals, and plants
- *Psuche*: The seat of the feelings, desires, affections, and aversions
- *Zoe*: Divine, eternal life

Jesus said to him, "I am the way, the truth, and the life. No one comes to the Father except through Me." (John 14:6)

A BRIEF HISTORY OF DEATH

- Adam introduced death by his sin. He was told, "You shall surely die" (Genesis 2:17).
- Death reigns for a time.
- All creation groans.
- Death will flee from them. This will happen during the great tribulation.
- Death and hell were thrown into the lake of fire.
- There shall be no more curse and no more tears.
- There will be no more death.

"And God will wipe away every tear from their eyes; there shall be no more death, nor sorrow, nor crying. There shall be no more pain, for the former things have passed away." (Revelation 21:4)

FEATURED CREATURES

John then describes the hideous creatures, and again language falls short in the attempt to paint a picture of these terrible beasts. John points out that the devil is their king (v. 11). This is confirmed by his name, which means "destroyer." This is a fitting description for the ruler of darkness.

SIXTH TRUMPET

Another horror is revealed with the sound of the sixth trumpet, when four angels bound at the Euphrates River are loosed to destroy a third of mankind. An army numbering 200 million now appears on the scene (v. 16), at a time when fully half of the human race has already been annihilated. This force is fueled by demonic power and is armed with the carnal reasoning of mankind.

Between World Wars I and II, it is estimated that 120 million people died. By contrast, the three plagues of fire, smoke, and brimstone result in the death of billions. Again, there is destruction on a worldwide scale.

DEADLY DEFIANCE

Despite the magnitude of these plagues, mankind remains defiant (v. 20). They refuse to stop worshiping demons and the idols their hands have created. In the great tribulation, Satan will be openly accepted while God is widely rejected.

The threads of civilization quickly unravel as murder, sexual immorality, and thefts abound (v. 21). Further, they refuse to repent of their sorceries, which comes from the Greek word that means drugs and magical remedies. Refusing to obey God results in a torrent of destructive behavior producing a literal hell on earth. This has been the goal of Satan from the beginning. The path of defiance leads to torment for mankind, while God's forgiveness leads to deliverance, freedom, and triumph.

14

ETERNAL WITNESSES

Revelation 10-11

"The Jewish Temple will be rebuilt on Temple Mount in Jerusalem and the daily sacrifices will begin again! How do we know this? Because both the Old and New Testaments testify to this fact. We don't know when this staggering transformation of Temple Mount will take place, but from all indications it should be very soon. In fact, the Temple must be rebuilt for certain other prophesied events to occur." – Dave Hunt[1]

I saw still another mighty angel coming down from heaven, clothed with a cloud. And a rainbow was on his head, his face was like the sun, and his feet like pillars of fire. (Revelation 10:1)

God is never left without a witness on earth. In the past, when the whole world was given over to evil, it came down to a family of eight who were building an ark. We now come to the point in

Revelation where four witnesses are supernaturally introduced between the sixth and seventh trumpets of judgment.

The first witness is a mighty angel (10:1–4). This angel may be a Christophany, which is an appearance of Jesus Christ outside of the incarnation. The visual description of this being lends credence to the Christophany theory, and the roar also alludes to the Lion of the tribe of Judah.

AND NOW A WORD FROM THE CREATOR

Satan is having a long-awaited field day on earth. Yes, he knows his time is short (Revelation 12:12), but sin has made him insane. And his lust for human destruction is insatiable. Onto this hellish stage comes a mighty angel with a message. John eats the message and digests its meaning, finding that it is both sweet and bitter (vv. 8–11).

Sir Walter Scott, an English poet, appropriately asked, "Does it not seem strange that Satan has been allowed for 6,000 years to wrap and twist his coils around the world and to work evil and spoil the work of God? Is it not a mystery why God, the God of righteousness and holiness, allows evil to go unpunished and His own people to be crushed and broken on every hand?"[2]

The message of the little book was sweet to the taste but bitter when its implications were fully considered. Metaphorically, this speaks of the gospel. The good news is attractive, but it can leave a sickening feeling for those who reject it.

TIME FOR THE TEMPLE

"The importance of the Temple Mount cannot be overestimated. Three of the world's great religions, Judaism, Islam, and Christianity hold the Mount in the highest regard. To Judaism and Islam, the Temple Mount is the holiest site in an area with many 'holy sites.' In addition, all three religions believe the 'Deliverer,' will someday come from the East through the Golden Gate onto the Temple Mount. Though the three religions agree that this spot is to witness future great events, they differ on what those events will be." – Don Stewart and Chuck Missler[3]

*Then I was given a reed like a measuring rod. And the angel stood, saying, "Rise and measure the temple of God, the altar, and those who worship there." (*Revelation 11:1)

On a terrible night in 70 AD, the Roman General Titus entered Jerusalem with his legions and proceeded to sack the city as punishment to the Jewish rebels. During the carnage, soldiers ransacked the Temple and destroyed it.

Jesus foresaw this night and predicted that not one stone would be left upon another (Mark 13:2). This was a fantastic, unbelievable prophecy to his followers. In its time, the Temple restoration by Herod was the largest construction project in the world.

Today, as Jesus promised, the Temple Mount is devoid of even one temple stone. Just off the familiar Western Wall, the Rabbi's Tunnel allows a firsthand look at a glimpse of the magnificence of the former Temple. One massive stone weighs over 500 tons, with amazing dimensions of 45 feet in length and nearly 10 feet in height.

Two temples have graced the Mount up to now: Solomon's and then Zerubbabel's, which was greatly expanded by Herod. Another temple will exist when the great tribulation engulfs the world. Further evidence the temple will be rebuilt is found in the New Testament prophecy that the Antichrist will exalt himself, demand worship, and seat himself as God in the temple (2 Thessalonians 2:3–4).

Obviously, the temple must exist for these things to take place. Furthermore, John is instructed to measure the Temple (v. 1). He is told not to measure the outer court because it is to be trampled underfoot by the Gentiles for 42 months—or as Jesus said, "until the time of the Gentiles be fulfilled" (Luke 21:24).

AGAINST ALL ODDS

It is estimated that John wrote Revelation in Patmos after 90 AD. At this time, no temple stood in Jerusalem because it had been destroyed by the troops of Titus more than two decades prior. This raises some hard questions about how John could obey this instruction.

WHY MUST THERE BE A TEMPLE?

The Temple Mount in Jerusalem is the core location on earth for the practice of Judaism. Author Joel Rosenberg calls it the "Epicenter," further describing it as the most coveted and dangerous piece of property on planet earth.[4]

Unfortunately, due to Israel's national disobedience, both of the previous temples were destroyed. Solomon's Temple was destroyed by the Babylonians in 586 BC, when Nebuchadnezzar laid siege to Jerusalem. As previously mentioned, the second Temple was destroyed by the Romans in 70 AD. A future temple is coming, but its construction is significantly complicated by the occupation of Muslims. In fact, the most notable landmark on the Temple Mount today is not Jewish at all; it is the gold dome of the Al-Aqsa Mosque, built in 705 AD.

"The rise and fall of the two temples were both predicted by God in the Old Testament (Isaiah, Jeremiah). In the ancient world, Jerusalem and its Temple Mount were center stage to many dramatic events. The time would come, however when this area would be neglected and profaned. Each of these structures were relatively short-lived. For the next two thousand years, the Temple Mount would lack any significant Jewish presence." – Don Stewart and Chuck Missler[5]

This holy place, the Temple Mount, literally chosen by God as His dwelling place on earth, has been treated badly by the very people it was meant to attract and bless. Antiochus of Syria profaned it by slaying a pig on the altar. Jewish historian Flavius Josephus records that Caius Caesar, (Caligula) sought to have his statue erected in the Temple. However, this treatment of the Temple by gentiles is tame compared to how God's chosen people have profaned the Temple and its precincts.

At one point, the neglect of God had deteriorated to such a point that the Scriptures had been lost even by those designated to assure their place in Israeli life. By accident, Hilkiah the priest came across the Book of the Law and brought it to the attention of the boy king Josiah (2 Kings 22).

By the time Jesus arrived on the scene, the temple precincts had degraded into a mall for merchants and moneychangers.

And He said to them, "It is written, 'My house shall be called a house of prayer,' but you have made it a 'den of thieves.'" (Matthew 21:13)

Ultimately, there will be another temple because it is required to complete the plan of God. There are also three Old Testament Scriptures which speak of the defilement of a future temple: Daniel 9:27, 11:31, and 12:11. None of them have been fulfilled—yet.

WHERE WILL THERE BE A TEMPLE?

The Temple Mount as expanded by Herod now occupies 40 acres of hotly contested real estate. It is unclear exactly where the original Temple, and thus the Holy of Holies, was located. For this reason, many Orthodox Jews will not set foot on the Mount because they fear treading on the spot where God's glory dwelt.

There are several theories about how the familiar golden-domed mosque could make way for the construction of the temple:

- An armed conflict that allows Israel to evict the Muslims from the Temple Mount. This would undoubtedly unleash a much wider war.
- A natural disaster that removes the mosque and makes way for Israel to proceed with construction.
- A negotiated agreement where Israel builds their temple either north or south of the Dome of the Rock.

None of these scenarios would be simple solutions, so the tension builds.

WHAT IF?

The Bible speaks of a coming world leader such as has never been seen before. His charisma and talent will lead the whole world to respect his leadership. What if he is the one to solve the conundrum of conflict between Israel and Islam that results in a peaceful agreement for temple construction? This would be a diplomatic miracle that understandably could propel this person to become a global leader. These could be the very events that introduce Antichrist to the world stage.

SUPER SAINTS ON THE SCENE

Contemporary culture has been focused on glorifying all manner of superheroes since the days of Superman in the 1950s. Many of the highest-grossing films of this century are about comic book heroes. For whatever reason, human beings seem to be focused on powerful heroes, and they will soon get a glimpse of the real thing.

At this time, two witnesses—God's superheroes—will appear on the scene for 1,260 days (v. 3). This three-and-a-half-year period is the same amount of time the Antichrist will be allowed to spew forth his blasphemous persecution and rhetoric. These witnesses are not named, but speculation has suggested Moses and Elijah. Whoever they are, the world will be powerless against them. They will have but one message for humanity: Repent.

Even the church could use more repentance today. Itching ears prefer a message of prosperity without repentance, but true exaltation begins with humility.

Throughout their brief ministry, these super saints will torment the inhabitants on earth with the truth, and during that time they will be indestructible.

Once their mission is fulfilled, the stage is set for an astonishing chain of events. First these two are slain (vv. 7–10). After three and a half days, they are raised from the dead and ascend to heaven while a worldwide audience watches in amazement (vv. 11–14).

This event is one of several technological advances that alert us to the times in which we live. Fulfillment of Revelation could not have taken place until these advances had taken place:

- Israel was established as a nation.
- Satellite television technology made global viewing of an event possible.
- Computer systems made a cashless society viable.
- Nuclear weapons were created that would allow the destruction of mankind.

Jesus predicted a time that fits the trumpet judgments of Revelation.

"And there will be signs in the sun, in the moon, and in the stars; and on the earth distress of nations, with perplexity, the sea and the waves roaring." (Luke 21:25)

"Distress with perplexity" is a dangerous combination, implying a severe situation with no foreseeable way out. With Islam and Israel locked in deadly conflict centered on the Temple Mount, there indeed seems to be no solution.

Zechariah correctly foresaw a day when this conflict would cause the lights to burn late into the night across the capitals of the world. Further, he prophesied that all the nations would agree to gather against Israel:

"And it shall happen in that day that I will make Jerusalem a very heavy stone for all peoples; all who would heave it away will surely be cut in pieces, though all nations of the earth are gathered against it." (Zechariah 12:3)

DRIVE THEM INTO THE SEA

Since that pivotal moment when the United Nations voted for Israel to be established as a nation, its "neighbors" have howled for the destruction of this Jewish state. More than merely complaining, they have repeatedly attacked. On May 14, 1948, the independent state of Israel was proclaimed as British rule in Palestine came to an end. Within 24 hours, Egypt, Jordan, Syria, Lebanon, and Iraq invaded. Armed conflict took place again in 1956, 1967, and 1973. Today, surrounding nations boldly and blatantly call for the total destruction of Israel.

"The commander of Iran's Revolutionary Guards said Monday that destroying arch-rival Israel has become an 'achievable goal' thanks to his country's technological advances. 'This sinister regime must be wiped off the map and this is no longer... a dream (but) it is an achievable goal,' Major General Hossein Salami said, quoted by the Guards' Sepah news site." – Quote from a widely reported 2019 AFP news story[6]

This is a typical rant against Israel from the radical side of Islam, and it's actually mild by some comparisons. At the United

Nations, Israel is a hated outcast. For example, in 2018 the UN issued 27 condemnations and 21 of them went to Israel. For comparison, China received zero and North Korea received one.

Zechariah is correct, the nations are gathering, and they're against Israel.

THE SEVENTH TRUMPET

This trumpet brings the third woe and the third witness: the witness of the elders (vv. 15–19). Here we see the close of mankind's reign and the advent of Christ's reign on earth. The twenty-four elders around the throne bear witness to the return of Jesus and the glory of God.

The Greek word for *wrath* here is interpreted as "indignation, a settled attitude of wrath." God's anger is not temperamental and unpredictable; it is holy indignation against sin. There will be either ruin or reward at the return of Christ; no middle ground exists. A "wait and see" attitude will not work.

These three witnesses to Christ's authority, power, and glory are the basis for our daily confidence in Jesus. When the world collapses around us and the order comes to "shelter in place," we can celebrate life rather than death knowing that our King is coming.

The name of the LORD is a strong tower; The righteous run to it and are safe. (Proverbs 18:10)

15

THE OVERCOMERS

Revelation 12

"From this point in Revelation, therefore, Satan and his hosts are excluded from the third heaven, the presence of God, although their temporary dominion over the second heaven (the sky) continues. Satan's defeat in heaven, however, is the occasion for him to be cast down to earth and explains the particular virulence of the Great Tribulation time." – John Walvoord[1]

Now a great sign appeared in heaven: a woman clothed with the sun, with the moon under her feet, and on her head a garland of twelve stars. Then being with child, she cried out in labor and in pain to give birth. And another sign appeared in heaven: behold, a great, fiery red dragon having seven heads and ten horns, and seven diadems on his heads. His tail drew a third of the stars of heaven and threw them to the earth. And the dragon stood before the woman who was ready to give birth, to devour her Child as soon as it was born. (Revelation 12:1–4)

John sees a vision (vv. 1–6) of fulfilled future prophecy. Two primary signs are seen here: the woman and the dragon.

The first sign is a woman representing the nation of Israel. The garland and the twelve stars represent the twelve tribes of Israel. The sun and moon mentioned here are often associated in Scripture with God's divine favor. The woman stands here in that position of blessing. The child she brings forth is the Christ. Jesus will rule the nations with a rod of iron when He returns.

The second sign, which is a dragon, appears again in verse 9. Revelation makes it perfectly clear that this fiery red dragon is Satan. This hideous creature has seven heads with seven crowns (diadems) sitting on each head and ten horns. This description is symbolic of Satan's dominion as prince (influencer) of this world. These ten horns represent the rulers who introduce a one-world government, which will be a ten-nation confederation led by the Antichrist.

As a third of the angels rebel with Satan, the dragon is poised to devour the child after its birth (v. 4). It should be no secret where the inspiration for late-term and after-birth abortion is found.

WAR IN HEAVEN

This war (vv. 7–12) represents a series of demonic conflicts related to Israel, coming to a climax with the eviction of Satan and his hordes from heaven.

So the great dragon was cast out, that serpent of old, called the Devil and Satan, who deceives the whole world; he was cast to the earth, and his angels were cast out with him. (Revelation 12:9)

This scene brings us an exclusive look at the fierce cosmic warfare that has existed from the beginning of time. Satan has been the dark nemesis of heaven since he made his fateful rebellion. Long ago his mutiny failed, but his manic efforts at offending God continue with the support of evil human beings—people like Herod, Haman, and Hitler—who always have the Jews in their crosshairs. Just as in the wilderness time during the days of Moses, God will protect and provide for His people.

God always ultimately protects and preserves His people. Still, the enemy has been able to wreak much havoc on the earth due to the cooperation of wicked people. Demonic accusations have been the culprit behind many wars and have manifested in racism, hatred, and murders. Satan knows that fallen human flesh is willing to compromise and cooperate with his hateful agenda. The good news is that salvation, the Kingdom of God, and the power of Christ finally are revealed in their fullness on the earth (v. 10a).

THREE KEYS TO THE KINGDOM

Overcome or succumb, that is the decision all believers on earth face at this time. First, overcomers believe in the power of the blood of Jesus (v. 11a). The blood cleanses the church of sin and also provides cleansing for our conscience.

It has become a common practice to send out our DNA for testing to determine genealogical background. Regardless of your physical DNA, all Christians have the blood of Christ in common. If Jesus is not the unifying component of the church, we will continue to divide ourselves over music types or carpet colors, basically valuing style over substance. We must remember and focus on what we have in common—the fact that we are covered by the blood of Jesus.

Next, the overcomers kept their testimonies, which is the power of their story. Overcomers must be willing to share their story. It is possible to argue over doctrine and dogma, but it is much more difficult to argue with a changed life. Finally, we see that overcomers love Jesus more than their lives (v. 11b). Narcissism, or the worship of self, is considered normal in today's world.

From India, we hear an astonishing story. A 27-year-old is suing his parents because they conceived him without his consent. Therefore, he believes they are obligated to pay for all his expenses over the duration of his entire life.[2] Sounds ridiculous, but it's not that far from the attitude of many. Some may even have such an attitude toward God since we live in a narcissistic selfie culture.

During the seven-year tribulation period, we find believers still overcoming by faith despite the severe persecution they suffer. Their testimony should serve as an example for the church today. My hope is that, in the Antichrist culture of our day, the example of these future saints will inspire us to live as victors rather than victims. In order to do that, we must believe that Christ is our victory.

16

MANIFESTATION OF THE BEAST

Revelation 13

"One of the best-known prophecies of the Tribulation is that "beast" or world leader popularly called the Antichrist, will have the ability to put his mark, "666," on the forehead and hand of people. To buy or sell during that period, you will need that mark. For the first time in 2000 years, it now technologically possible to enforce such a system." – Tim LaHaye[1]

And I stood upon the sand of the sea, and saw a beast rise up out of the sea, having seven heads and ten horns, and upon his horns ten crowns, and upon his heads the name of blasphemy. (Revelation 13:1 KJV)

Revelation 13 brings the main characters of the great tribulation onto the scene, including the Antichrist, who is an evil incarnation. He is first called a "beast" (v. 1), a hideous creature rising up out of humanity to deceive the world. His wickedness will be cloaked initially while he emerges as a peacemaker. Midway through the tribulation, this camouflage will be stripped away. His true nature will emerge, but not before he has completely rearranged the world's order, politics, and economy. This will be a world unrecognizable by any previous standard.

Ancient borders will be erased in the name of world peace. Currencies will be abolished while calendars and holidays will be altered. Easter and Christmas? Adios. The Fourth of July? Forget that. It is a new day with a new world order. As Daniel predicted, this "man of sin" will demand a thoroughly secular society (Daniel 7:25). That is, until he doesn't. At some point, his demands will dramatically change.

COMPLETE CONTEMPT TOWARD GOD

On each of the seven heads, there is a blasphemous name. Seven is the Hebrew number for completion. Thus, this is complete contempt towards God. *Blasphemy* is literally "the prostitution of a sacred name to an unholy purpose."

In John's vision, there appears to be a revival of the Roman Empire symbolized by the seven heads representing the seven hills of Rome. This indicates that a world-governing empire will rise and rule again as others have done before with ferocity (Babylonians), tyranny (Medo-Persians), swiftness (Greeks), and ruthlessness (Rome).

The ten horns represent ten kings. The crowns represent ruling authority (v. 1b) that is granted by the dragon. This alliance will form a ten-nation confederation. The confederation will be one component of a fourfold system that ushers in worldwide false unity.

- One-World Government (13:7)
- One-World Leader (13:2; Daniel 7:4–7)
- One-World Religion (13:8)
- One-World Economy (13:16–18)

The Antichrist will suffer a mortal wound (v. 3) that will be healed. This stunning phenomenon will lead the world to wonder and then to worship. Paul referred to this season when he foresaw the coming of the lawless one who would introduce satanic signs and wonders as his calling card (2 Thessalonians 2:9–12). The world will revel in his gifts and charisma, rejecting God and bringing on a "strong delusion" so that they believe a lie. Worship of this beast will take place (v. 4–9) as true believers are subjected to severe persecution.

Note the objects of this blasphemy: God, heaven, and the saints who have gone there.

It opened its mouth to blaspheme God, and to slander his name and his dwelling place and those who live in heaven. It was given power to wage war against God's holy people and to conquer them. And it was given authority over every tribe, people, language and nation. All inhabitants of the earth will worship the beast—all whose names have not been written in the Lamb's book of life, the Lamb who was slain from the creation of the world. (Revelation 13:6–8 NIV)

Also observe in verse 8 a perverse and reverse Pentecost. Satan is the great imitator, not a creator. He inspires every tribe and nation to worship the beast in all languages, the satanic opposite of what took place in the second chapter of Acts.

IRON MAN HAS CLAY FEET

Mankind has always entertained a phenomenal obsession with superheroes. Romans, Greeks, Egyptians, and Babylonians all promoted a pantheon of various otherworldly gods. Their gods were sometimes in competition with each other for astral achievement and human affection.

God has placed eternity in the hearts of man (Ecclesiastes 3:11). For that reason, most empires were governed with a combination of secular power and strange spiritual practices.

Contemporary western culture is no different now that America is in a post-Christian era. As previously noted, superheroes are increasingly embraced on a passionate level by people across the globe, and especially in the US. From Superman to the Avengers, there is a social and spiritual fascination with the supernatural traits of these fantasy characters.

What if a true superman appears on planet earth? That is what takes place at this point in the book of Revelation, but this superhero is not helpful, good, or holy.

Another beast appears (v. 11) having the appearance of a lamb, but in fact it is under the influence of the devil. This spiritual leader will tickle the ears of the people promoting a one-world religious system (vv. 12, 13). He will sway the people through deceptive signs and lying wonders. This false teacher (vv. 14, 15) will duplicate signs similar to those of the "two witnesses" (Revelation 11). This is the same type of trickery perpetrated by Pharaoh's sorcerers, who performed some of the miracles that Moses performed (Exodus 7). However, this will be on a much wider and more dramatic scale.

The Antichrist will perpetuate his deception of mankind by encouraging worship of the beast. The false prophet will be granted the power to give life to the image or statue. This image will apparently be able to speak. It will also be able to hand out a death sentence to those who refuse to worship the beast.

Every person on the planet will be forced to take a special mark. Without it, no one will be able to buy or sell (vv. 16-17). People will be faced with the unimaginable choice between feeding their family and obeying the Lord.

FOUR PIVOT POINTS

Jesus left His followers with a stiff neck as they gazed upward into heaven (Acts 1:9-11). Ever since that moment, believers have been waiting for and expecting His return.

Now twenty-one centuries have passed, giving today's church the benefit of perspective. It is clear from this viewpoint that the fulfillment of prophecy and the return of Jesus could not have taken place until these four pivotal pieces were in place.

ATOMIC WEAPONS

Worldwide destruction needed to be possible because Jesus said mankind would be on the verge of an extinction-level event.

"And unless those days were shortened, no flesh would be saved; but for the elect's sake, those days will be shortened." (Matthew 24:22)

This was not possible until the advent of nuclear weapons in the 1940s.

SATELLITE TECHNOLOGY

It must be possible for the whole world to watch the death and resurrection of the two witnesses.

For three and a half days some from every people, tribe, language and nation will gaze on their bodies and refuse them burial. (Revelation 11:9 NIV)

Satellite television did not exist until 1962.

CASHLESS SOCIETY

The infamous mark of the beast (Revelation 13:16–18) could only be possible with the invention of microchip implants, sophisticated computers, and banking technology.

This level of worldwide coordination was not possible until the 1970s but has become further refined in the past 40 years. Both identity theft of credit cards and the viral dangers associated with paper currency will motivate the advent of a cashless society. However, the most powerful underlying cause will be the desire for total control by a one-world government.

ISRAEL MUST EXIST

While the church is absent from Revelation after chapter 3 (say that out loud, then ask yourself why that's the case), Israel is again center stage, including the descent of the new Jerusalem (21:2).

From the night in 70 AD when the Romans legions of Titus torched Jerusalem and the Jews were subsequently evicted from Israel, the great diaspora took place. For nearly 2,000 years, the Jews were without a homeland, but not without a future. They are indispensable to both Scripture and history.

"The Jews started it all – and by 'it' I mean so many of the things we care about, the underlying values that make all of us, Jew and Gentile, believer and atheist, tick. Without the Jews, we would see the world through different eyes, hear with different ears, even feel with different feelings ... We would think with a different mind, interpret all our experiences differently, draw different conclusions from the things that befall us. And we would set a different course for our lives." – Thomas Cahill[2]

Israel became a nation again on May 14, 1948. Tim LaHaye called this event a super sign, a major piece of the prophetic puzzle firmly and clearly put into place.

THE ROOTS OF REBELLION

It did not take long for mankind to reject the lessons that were taught by the great flood of Noah. Soon, a false system of worship was birthed on the plains of Shinar. Here, the first of many world dictators raised his fist in rebellion.

In blatant defiance of God, Nimrod constructed a tower with the intent of reaching heaven. Astrology, sorcery, and an entire false religion were centered around this structure.

Have you wondered where traditions such as Lent came from?

From Babylon a system of religion developed. This religious system was initiated by Semiramis, who was Nimrod's wife. We can consider her to be the first high priestess of idolatrous worship. According to legend, her son Tammuz was killed by a wild boar.

Further, after his mother wept for forty days, he was raised back to life.

Here we find the roots of "mother and child" worship. The forty days of Lent are rooted in this cultic story. After the forty days of Lent, the feast of Ishtar was celebrated with the exchanging of Ishtar eggs, symbolic of new life in the spring.

Bible scholar Dr. H. A. Ironside traces the other remnants of this ancient legend that has manifested to this very day:

"When Constantine came to the throne and the first pope assumed the title Pontifex Maximus, all those heathen associations and ceremonies that had their beginning with Nimrod—the worship of the Queen of the Heavens, the eating of the wafer, the doctrine of purgatory, the wearing of vestments, and the observance of a thousand and one lesser mysteries—all these were brought into the church, and for a thousand years they prevailed over all Europe. Thus the Roman Catholic Church with all its doctrines and practices came into existence." - Dr. H. A. Ironside[3]

The abominable mother-son cult is memorialized by the prophet Ezekiel who is given access to a progressive series of adulterous practices in the very heart of Israel, the Temple.

And He said to me, "Turn again, and you will see greater abominations that they are doing." So He brought me to the door of the north gate of the LORD's house; and to my dismay, women were sitting there weeping for Tammuz. (Ezekiel 8:13–14)

Nimrod was a prototype—the first of a series of self-appointed evil leaders who presumed to be like the Most High. As Merrill Unger observed, Nimrod was the first of many. But we will soon see the last of the false world leaders.

"History, since the fall of man, has been an unbroken attestation of the ominous fact of evil powers in human rulers. Perhaps the most solemn demonstration of the utter barbarity and horrible cruelty and wickedness of men energized by demon power, has been reserved for the boasted civilization and enlightenment of the twentieth century. Hitler, the demon-energized and demon-directed scourge of Europe has come and gone, leaving behind a trail of agonized suffering and a stage of chaos upon which atheistic communism is determined to perpetrate even greater evils." – Merril Unger[4]

THE SHADOW ILLUMINATED

The Old Testament is frequently called a shadow of things to come (Colossians 2:17; Hebrews 8:5, 10:1). Therefore, a poverty of understanding about Old Testament events will likely result in confusion concerning New Testament revelation. When it comes to understanding the book of Revelation, no prophetic book is more vital than the book of Daniel.

This book is a scriptural treasure map which lays a path to Revelation. X marks the spot as the hope of the ages—final redemption from the corporate human nightmare of sin—is laid out for us. The revelations given to Daniel are so powerful and informative that a review of merely the highlights will contribute to a clearer understanding of the Apocalypse.

DANIEL CHAPTER 2

A dream that reveals the rise and fall of world empires.

"We're all watching rather sadly - we who know Christ - the fall of the United States of America. As sad as it is, it shouldn't really shock us. The reason is because it has always been and always will be the lot of nations, nations of the world, that the kingdoms of men will go the way of all flesh and ultimately end in collapse and ruin. Anything based on the might of man, anything established on the wisdom of man will suffer the same kind of deterioration that man himself suffers since the fall." – John MacArthur[5]

Daniel described the dream of King Nebuchadnezzar detailing a great image that represented the kingdom of Babylon, as well as those that would succeed Babylon. These kingdoms are laid out in decreasing order of value.

- Head of fine gold—Babylon—This refers to King Nebuchadnezzar's preoccupation with gold.
- Chest and arms of silver—Medo-Persian Empire—The Medes required that their taxes be paid in silver and they literally filled their coffers with tons and tons of silver.
- Belly and thigh of bronze—the Greek Empire of Alexander—When you saw a Greek soldier, he would have had on a helmet of brass or bronze, a breastplate of brass, and he would be carrying a shield and a sword both made out of brass.
- Legs of iron—the Roman Empire—This empire endured

an east-west schism between Rome and Constantinople, where the legs represent the Eastern Roman Empire and the Western Roman Empire.

- Feet and toes of iron and clay—a coming ten-nation confederacy—This will be a revived Roman Empire, constituted by a grouping of European nations.
- A great stone strikes the image, becomes a mountain, and fills the whole earth. At the end of days, Jesus, who is the rock, will strike this image and overcome it. He will then institute His true and final world-governing kingdom.

DANIEL CHAPTER 7

A series of animals are envisioned in a dream of Daniel during the reign of King Belshazzar (Daniel 7:1–6).

- A leopard symbolized the blitz-like speed with which the Grecian General Alexander the Great swept through other nations.
- The bear represents the brute power that the Medio-Persian Empire exhibited in their conquests.
- A lion with eagle's wings signified the Babylonian Empire.

A fourth terrible beast (7:7) is unique due to what arises from it.

DANIEL CHAPTER 8

A fierce king will arise with the power of the Antichrist. He will assault Israel and even challenge Prince Jesus (vv. 11, 25), but he will be defeated at the battle of Armageddon.

DANIEL CHAPTER 9

First, we should take special note of Daniel 9:26, "Messiah shall be cut off, but not for Himself"—a clear prophecy about the sacrifice of Jesus on the cross. The book of Daniel has proven accurate before and it will continue to do so.

The Antichrist and the final seven-year tribulation are described as the events swirl around the epicenter of Jerusalem. This monster will appear to negotiate a Mideast peace treaty that allows Israel to rebuild its temple, establishing sacrifices and worship. Suddenly, after three and a half years, the Antichrist will invade and take over the temple. This leads to the ultimate abomination: he will require the world to worship him and his image. This sets off a heavenly trip wire of judgment, the intrusion of a violated border that cannot be tolerated.

Scripture demands that Israel exist as a nation when the curtain is systematically drawn back, revealing the inevitable events explained by John's grand vision.

"Israel is a miracle nation. It was born by a miracle, it lived by a miracle, and it has been preserved by the miraculous hand of God all through history. That after 1500 years without a homeland this dispersed people could be gathered back into a holy land in this century, and recognized as an official nation in 1948, is itself a miracle. Historians tell us that no other nationality has been able to survive extinction after 500 years of being removed from its homeland." — Tim LaHaye[6]

DANIEL CHAPTER 11

Exalting and glorifying himself in the deceptive power of Satan, the Antichrist utters blasphemies to the God of heaven. Speculation about the identity of the Antichrist will be fruitless despite the best of efforts of Hollywood and misguided "prophecy experts." Who he is remains a mystery for now, but he will eventually be revealed (2 Thessalonians 2:3).

DANIEL CHAPTER 12

A great glimpse is given of how the times of man will conclude. Divine wisdom is given for those who are wise.

And many of those who sleep in the dust of the earth shall awake,

Some to everlasting life,

Some to shame and everlasting contempt.

Those who are wise shall shine

Like the brightness of the firmament,

And those who turn many to righteousness

Like the stars forever and ever. (Daniel 12:2–3)

But as wonderful as it is, this is only a brief glimpse.

And he said, "Go your way, Daniel, for the words are closed up and sealed till the time of the end." (Daniel 12:9)

The magnificent prophecy of Daniel compliments the sealed scrolls of Revelation. In the current time, we find ourselves wedged in the middle of tremendous heavenly parentheses, waiting for the drumbeat of the apocalypse to increase in tempo as it reaches for the final crescendo.

In the meantime, how are we to understand the place of America, unmentioned in the biblical record of nations? There is a brilliant observation which is purported to have been written over 200 years ago, and is most often attributed to Professor Alexander Tytler.[7] The quote was said to describe the general way of nations. Applied to America, this would of course predict where the United States would eventually fall:

- From bondage to spiritual faith
- From spiritual faith to great courage
- From courage to liberty
- From liberty to abundance
- From abundance to selfishness
- From selfishness to complacency
- From complacency to apathy
- From apathy to dependence
- From dependence back into bondage

While the origin of this quote is disputed, it's popular for a reason —it's generally accurate.

Could this cycle be the reason for the absence of America in prophecy? That we will see some kind of major downfall in the near future? Or could it be that we will see a wide and genuine revival followed by the rapture? If that happened, it could take America largely out of the picture before the events of Revelation.

In either case, the day is coming when the door of grace will begin to swing shut. The church is on the clock to work while it is the day—before the dreaded and melancholy words of Jeremiah are true for the final generation.

The harvest is past, the summer is ended, and we are not saved. (Jeremiah 8:20 KJV)

17

GRAPES OF WRATH

Revelation 14:14-20

"Satan has always tried to masquerade as God. Here the dragon will try to masquerade as God the Father, while the Antichrist will masquerade as the Son. At this point in the Tribulation, all the dreams that people have expressed for a one-world religion will be fulfilled—but it will be demonic and blasphemous." – Skip Heitzig[1]

Then I looked, and behold, a white cloud, and on the cloud sat One like the Son of Man, having on His head a golden crown, and in His hand a sharp sickle. (Revelation 14:14)

The timing of God's wrath (vv. 14–16) brings forth a judgment scene where Jesus is preparing to sweep the earth clean of all evil. The harvest here is not the gathering of good wheat but rather the tares—the children of the wicked one that Jesus referred to in Matthew 13:40–42.

THERE IS A LIMIT

God has placed a limit on the amount of iniquity He will tolerate, and in this passage, we find that the cup of evildoing is now full. The harvest is ripe because the time for God's judgment has come (v. 15).

Consider the human condition and how offensive it must be to God. Abortion, abuse, addiction, adultery, alcoholism—and those are just the tip of the iceberg. The list of man's wickedness continues down to unspeakable depths. The time is quickly approaching when God will say, "Enough!" At just such a time, we are told (v. 15) that an angel comes out of the temple in heaven to declare that the reaping on earth will begin.

There is a biblical precedent for God drawing a line in the sand for mankind. He sometimes sets boundaries that bring about inescapable consequences when crossed.

DON'T TOUCH

Adam and Eve were instructed not to eat of the tree of the knowledge of good and evil (Genesis 2:17). The inevitable consequence was for death to reign.

DON'T GATHER

Post-flood, mankind was instructed to scatter and repopulate the earth (Genesis 9:1). They did the opposite, gathering on the plains of Shinar to make their own name great and build their temple to heaven (Genesis 11:4). The Lord came to earth to observe this project and concluded that if this disobedience was allowed to proceed, evil would again take over as it had before the flood.

Human language was confounded, and it has been that way ever since.

In the case of Revelation 14, mankind's cumulative unrepentant sin has reached the point of no return and global judgment unfolds.

THE EXTENT OF GOD'S WRATH

The object of God's wrath is the vine (vv. 17-18), the false vine of the Antichrist, representing the apostate church and apostate Israel. The location of this great reckoning is the valley of Armageddon (16:16), located west of the Jordan River and 38 miles southwest of the Sea of Galilee.

Ezekiel describes this same scene (Ezekiel 39:8–16). In fact, the prophet tells us that it takes seven months to bury the dead and seven years to burn up all the weapons used in this final battle.

18

THE FINALITY OF DIVINE WRATH

Revelation 15–16

"Of all the things that will surprise us at the resurrection, this I believe will surprise us most: that we did not love Christ more before we died." – J.C. Ryle[1]

Then I saw another sign in heaven, great and marvelous: seven angels having the seven last plagues, for in them the wrath of God is complete. (Revelation 15:1)

On the brink of the coming seven bowl judgments, the saints of the tribulation are standing in victory and sharing the song of Moses (Exodus 15). This song is also known as the song of the Lamb, who has delivered His church from the bondage and penalty of sin. In verse 4, there is a reference to the time when Christ reigns on the earth for a thousand years.

The temple of the tabernacle (vv. 5–7) refers to the holy of holies where the ark of the testimony (covenant) resides, which also appeared earlier in Revelation (11:19).

Each angel has a golden band, or sash, across their chest. They are adorned in priestly garments, because their task is a holy one. Jesus, our high priest, previously appeared with a golden sash, (1:13).

God's glory is manifested as the temple is filled with smoke (15:8). This recalls Moses' experience on Mount Sinai (Exodus 19:18) when the Law was declared and the judgment explained for those who failed to obey.

SEVEN BOWLS, SEVEN PLAGUES

The final seven plagues come in the form of bowl judgments (16:1–21). These bowl or vial judgments are the final judgments of the tribulation period, and they will be the most severe judgments the world has ever seen.

THE FIRST BOWL

Tribulation saints will be immune from this plague of painful sores that break out on any who have the mark of the beast and worship its image.

THE SECOND BOWL

One-third of all sea life had been destroyed at the second trumpet (8:9). Now, all oceans turn to blood and rest of sea life is eradicated. The effect that dead oceans have upon the remaining life on earth cannot be overstated.

THE THIRD BOWL

Fresh water is the next casualty when the rivers and springs also are turned to blood (16:4–5). Unimaginable misery results and the days of man are ticking down rapidly.

THE FOURTH BOWL

"And the sun was allowed to scorch people with fire. They were seared by the intense heat," (16:8–9 NIV). Despite the increasing tempo and ferocity of judgment, the inhabitants of earth refuse to repent and glorify God. Instead, they curse His name.

THE FIFTH BOWL

The fifth of the seven bowls brings great darkness. The pain and suffering will intensify to the point that people gnaw their tongues in agony (16:10–11). And yet, the followers of Antichrist will not repent (v. 11).

THE SIXTH BOWL

The curtain between the spiritual world is being ripped open when John sees three unclean spirits "that looked like frogs" coming from the mouths of Satan, the Antichrist, and the False Prophet (v. 13). They perform miracles that deceive world leaders (v. 14). The way is opened for the kings of the east to cross the Euphrates for a final battle. Under the demonic influence, "the armies assemble together to the place that in Hebrew is called Armageddon" (v. 16).

THE SEVENTH BOWL

The seventh bowl brings an earthquake so severe that "no earthquake like it has ever occurred since mankind has been on earth, so tremendous was the quake" (v. 18 NIV). Jerusalem is split into three parts, islands are flooded, cities collapse, and mountains vanish (v. 20). Huge hailstones, "each weighing about a hundred pounds, fell on people" (v. 21 NIV).

By this point in the great tribulation, there will be a complete breakdown of the earth's protective ozone layer. This is the ultimate in climate change. Ozone depletion will magnify all of the effects of ultraviolet rays on human health, including sunburn, skin cancer, cataracts, and worse. Scorching heat reigns in an atmosphere now devoid of cooling breezes and refreshing rain. Remember, the winds have ceased, which will result in a halt to the evaporation and hydration process on earth.

Despite all these horrific events, men will continue to blaspheme rather than turn to the living God. A ringing warning from Jesus closes this chapter.

"Behold, I am coming as a thief. Blessed is he who watches, and keeps his garments, lest he walk naked and they see his shame." (Revelation 16:15)

19

THE SCARLET HARLOT

Revelation 17

"As the major lines of prophetic revelation concerning the tribulation period have been surveyed it becomes obvious that the revelation of God's program for this period constitutes one of the major sections of prophetic study. The program for Israel, for the Gentiles, for the program of Satan, all reach a climax in that time immediately preceding the second advent of Christ." – J. Dwight Pentecost[1]

Then one of the seven angels who had the seven bowls came and talked with me, saying to me, "Come, I will show you the judgment of the great harlot who sits on many waters." (Revelation 17:1)

The great harlot that is depicted here is the false church of the tribulation period. She is called a harlot because of her unfaithfulness to her husband, Jesus Christ. The false church will be the fullest manifestation of apostasy. This is a clear warning to the modern church, which is in danger of playing the harlot.

God considers the rejection of His authority in our lives to be spiritual harlotry. The United Methodist Church experienced a split in 2019 due to a vote in their conference concerning homosexuality.

"America's second-largest Protestant denomination, the United Methodist Church, is set to split, as the church's top policy-making body voted Thursday to maintain prohibitions on homosexuality and to expel gay pastors. Today's vote at the UMC's General Conference in St. Louis—delayed by filibusters, amendments, and other tactics by progressives—comes after two compromise options were rejected by narrow margins [53% – 46%]" – Jay Michaelson[2]

How could the margin be so narrow? It is because the church is now embracing the same spiritual fornication that we find here in the great harlot, the false church of the tribulation period. As His church, we are betrothed to Christ, but far too often the church is found in the arms of other lovers.

- Lust of the flesh
- Lust of the eyes
- Pride of life

Do not love the world or the things in the world. If anyone loves the world, the love of the Father is not in him. For all that is in the world—the lust of the flesh, the lust of the eyes, and the pride of life —is not of the Father but is of the world. (1 John 2:15 – 16)

The only remedy is repentance—to return to your first love by doing the will of the Father, according to His word.

THE HARLOT

The great harlot has been a confounding figure for centuries. She is very powerful as she sits astride a system that has global impact (Revelation 17:15). She sits on many waters. Those who follow are intoxicated by her. Arrayed in purple and scarlet, she harkens back to Roman royalty and rank (v. 4).

She represents a monstrous, ecumenical system that John calls "Mystery Babylon." This is a spiritual system of false religion which leads the masses away from the one true God. The tentacles of Mystery Babylon trace back to Genesis 10, as discussed earlier. Here, Nimrod—only four generations removed from Noah— established a city. The purpose of this city was to magnify man and degrade God. The city was called Babel, and later on, Babylon.

This first major evidence of secular humanism was just the start. Babylon also became the home to a mystery religion that spawned a whole host of false offspring under a variety of brands. This idolatrous feminine matriarch figure is often portrayed as a goddess mother with her mythical male offspring. We see this same setup over the centuries throughout multiple cultures.

- Semiramis in Babel, whose son was Tammuz
- Ishtar in Nineveh
- Isis in Egypt, where her son was known as Horus
- Ashtoreth in Egypt

- Aphrodite in Greece, with Eros
- Venus and her son Cupid in Rome
- Isi and Iswara in India
- Artemis of the Greeks became known as Diana of the Romans, whose followers Paul riled up at Ephesus.

Now when they heard this, they were full of wrath and cried out, saying, "Great is Diana of the Ephesians!" (Acts 19:28)

Therefore, John identifies her as, "MYSTERY, BABYLON THE GREAT, THE MOTHER OF HARLOTS" (Revelation 17:5) who is seated on a scarlet beast. Scarlet is the color of the beast, the color of both Satan (Revelation 12:3) and sin (Isaiah 1:18a).

Sin is like a parasite which hopelessly stains the soul of mankind. When Jesus died for a guilty race, He made it possible for the stain to be made as white as snow. But the scarlet harlot refuses peace with God. Instead, she has taken a symbol of shame and used it as a sinful badge of honor.

Babylon is not a geographical location but a spirit of rebellion, "Mystery Babylon" (v. 5). Babylon is derived from the word *babel*, which is associated with confusion. The religion of the great harlot will be one of turmoil, inspired by the author of confusion and the father of lies, the devil. This will be a man-made religion with no absolutes—a religion in which people fashion God in their own image.

On the head of this woman we find these words, "THE MOTHER OF HARLOTS AND OF THE ABOMINATIONS OF THE EARTH." Her illicit, spiritual "intercourse" with the world's system is contrary to the behavior of the true church of Christ.

She is found intoxicated on the blood of the saints and the martyrs of Jesus. She has fully embraced the Antichrist's spirit and message, which has been promoted by the False Prophet (Revelation 13:12–18). The secret of the harlot is now revealed (v. 8). The beast is the one carrying the woman.

In order to have the world's support, the church will always have to appease the Antichrist's system. So it is never a good thing when the world starts supporting the church.

The seven heads here are seven mountains (v. 9) where the harlot resides. The city of Rome is situated on seven hills. This has caused speculation among scholars that the Roman Catholic Church, aligned with some mainline protestants, may be at the helm of the false church during the tribulation. There are also seven kings. Five of these kings (kingdoms) had already passed away at the time of John's vision. However, one was present in John's day, and one was yet to come.

One perspective is that the past five kingdoms are Egypt, Assyria, Babylon, Persia, and Greece. In John's day, the present kingdom would have been the Roman Empire. That would leave the future kingdom as the kingdom of the beast.

If this verse refers to specific individual kings or rulers of the Roman Empire, they would be Julius Caesar, Tiberius, Caligula, Claudius, and Nero. The sixth would be Domitian, who was alive when John wrote the book of Revelation. The seventh would be the Antichrist.

Both views end with the same concluding scene: a temporary rule by the beast.

This monstrous leader will continue for a short time (v. 10b), only seven years, as he rules over the revived Roman Empire of the last days (Daniel 9:27). Daniel prophesied that this confederation will be ruled by the Antichrist for 3 ½ years, "a time and times and half a time." During this season, unbelievers will experience a demonically inspired unity (v. 13a). Their worldly solidarity, built on a false foundation, will crumble before the Lamb (v. 14).

TRUE OR FALSE?

Despite appearances to the contrary on earth, God is in control (v. 17) as the nations turn against the harlot and she is destroyed by the very allies that once supported her. False religion results in false security for the scarlet harlot.

What distinguishes a true church from a false on? There are three questions we should ask.

1. WHAT DOES THE CHURCH BELIEVE ABOUT JESUS?

Some so-called Christian churches seek to lower the status of Christ. This is a red flag, non-negotiable issue. We cannot allow Jesus to be treated as an equal to other so-called deities. This is religious pluralism—the belief that there are many different ways to God.

Jesus said to him, "I am the way, the truth, and the life. No one comes to the Father except through Me." (John 14:6)

2. WHAT DOES THE CHURCH BELIEVE ABOUT THE WORD OF GOD?

Sola scriptura is Latin for "by Scripture alone." Is the Bible diluted and stripped of its authority, or is the Bible exalted as inerrant and supreme in authority?

All Scripture is given by inspiration of God, and is profitable for doctrine, for reproof, for correction, for instruction in righteousness, that the man of God may be complete, thoroughly equipped for every good work. (2 Timothy 3:16–17)

3. WHAT HAVE THEY DONE WITH EACH OTHER?

The true church must not only hear the Word, but act upon it, because faith without works is dead.

My little children, let us not love in word or in tongue, but in deed and in truth. (1 John 3:18)

As the church, let us resist the powerful spirit of harlotry until it is finally and fully extinguished.

20

BABYLON IS FALLEN

Revelation 18

"Where is the church during the seven year Tribulation, as outlined in Revelation 4-19? If posttribulationism were correct, you would expect to see the church mentioned as being on earth during this time. But that is not the picture one sees in Revelation 4:19." – Robert Gromacki[1]

After these things I saw another angel coming down from heaven, having great authority, and the earth was illuminated with his glory. And he cried mightily with a loud voice, saying, "Babylon the great is fallen, is fallen, and has become a dwelling place of demons, a prison for every foul spirit, and a cage for every unclean and hated bird!" (Revelation 18:1–2)

The reign of mankind is now coming to a close. Following the demise of the false apostate church, we now have the downfall of "Babylon the great." Babylon the great is related to but distinct from "Mystery Babylon," which is the false religious system Satan has instituted on the earth. Some speculate that Babylon the great is only a world-system. However, we see that Babylon is both an ideology and the geographic location of a certain city.

At this point, the return of Christ is at hand. Before His return, however, the way must be prepared through the destruction of Babylon. Any and all reliance upon mankind's resources, religion, and remedies must be abandoned. Worldwide reliance upon Christ alone will replace mankind's reliance upon Babylon.

In this monumental moment, we find four voices speaking.

THE VOICE OF CONDEMNATION

First, we find the evil rebellious spirit of Babylon has consumed the false church (v. 1 – 3). This same spirit is set to utterly destroy the political power of the Antichrist. Babylon represents "every foul spirit, and a cage for every unclean and hated bird" (v. 2). This is a reference to satanic activity, which will be prevalent and worldwide in the last days.

While some scholars believe that the ancient city of Babylon will be rebuilt, others suggest that the use of the city's name here is symbolic—it may well be speaking of another city. I believe this to be the case for two reasons.

1. After Cyrus the Great conquered Babylon on October 12, 539 BC, God declared the beauty and glory of Babylon would never exist again (Isaiah 13:17–22).
2. In Revelation 11:8, God refers to Jerusalem by another name, calling Jerusalem "Sodom and Egypt" in a spiritual sense. So there is precedent for God referring to one city by the name of another well-known city when they are both under the same type of spirit. What is certain here is

that there is a strong condemnation against the spirit of Babylon and those who are enchanted by it.

THE VOICE OF SEPARATION

The wrath that Babylon has stored up is now being paid in full. She has condemned herself.

The voice here is reflective of Jeremiah's prophecy (Jeremiah 51:6–9) which calls for separation of God's people. He tells God's people to come out from underneath this Babylonian system of inequalities, for her time of judgment has come.

The arrogance of Babylon is seen again. This is the same arrogant sentiment that permeates culture, entertainment, and politics today. As in ancient Sodom, people will persist in an ungodly state, resisting Him until it's too late.

Her judgment takes place quickly in one day (v. 8). In a short period, Babylon will be destroyed. This destruction could refer to a sudden nuclear attack (v. 9, 10).

It is possible that a nuclear attack against America may be the opportunity for Gog (Russia) to launch an invasion against Israel, as predicted in Ezekiel 38 and 39. It is interesting that America (the west) is not mentioned as a world power or ally of Israel during the Tribulation period. With the impending judgment of Babylon so near, God warns His people just as He did in the days of Noah and Lot. He does the same with the modern church today, warning us to prepare for the rapture. God is just, and He always gives plenty of fair warning. This time is no different. The clarion call is clear to the tribulation church: "Come out of her (Babylon)" (v. 4).

THE VOICE OF LAMENTATION

Do not be confused by the third voice lamenting over the demise of Babylon. The concern is not for their grievous sin, but rather the loss of riches. This is a narcissistic cry, and here we see the wailing of a soul consumed with self.

THE VOICE OF CELEBRATION

The final voice is one of celebration. As the whole world mourns, heaven rejoices (vv. 20–24).

The world mourns because they refuse to repent and therefore continue to be deceived. A drug-addicted world will be simple to deceive as people will not be in their right minds. The more a society is given over to *pharmakeia* and recreational drug use, the more its citizens are capable of acting in a self-destructive manner. Despite the terrible conditions on earth, heaven rejoices because God is finally avenging the shed blood of His prophets and saints.

So we find that Babylon falls because the gods of this age must be dethroned before Christ can reign. So it is in our lives—the idols of Babylon must fall before Jesus can take his rightful position on the throne of our hearts.

What does it mean to "come out from among them?" Remember, God does not call His church out of the world, but rather to live obediently in the world and faithfully represent the gospel. Separation, then, has more to do with what is in the heart of the Christian than what is outside the church. A litmus test for the true state of one's heart is to identify what the soul longs for. Is it the sensation and security of Babylon and its physical promises? Or is it the solid rock of kingdom promises?

21

ENTER THE LION

Revelation 19

"To fall in love with God is the greatest romance; to seek him the greatest adventure; to find him, the greatest human achievement." – St. Augustine of Hippo[1]

"Let us be glad and rejoice and give Him glory, for the marriage of the Lamb has come, and His wife has made herself ready." And to her it was granted to be arrayed in fine linen, clean and bright, for the fine linen is the righteous acts of the saints. Then he said to me, "Write: 'Blessed are those who are called to the marriage supper of the Lamb!'" And he said to me, "These are the true sayings of God." (Revelation 19:7–9)

The wait is nearly over. The hope of the saints is preparing to take centerstage. Jesus is prepared to return. This is such a great moment that the Holy Spirit reserved a unique word for it. This is the only usage of this word in the New Testament, and it is used four times in this passage for emphasis: *Hallelujah!*

Hallelujah means "praise the Lord!" Praise the Lord for:

1. Redemption (v. 1)
2. Vengeance (v. 2)
3. Greatness (v. 5)
4. Power (v. 6b)

HERE COMES THE GROOM

At some level, we have all experienced the high moments of a wedding day: the preparation, the elaborate setting, and, finally, standing for the grand entrance of the bride. She will never look more glamorous as she stars in the largest social event of her life.

TRADITIONS, TRADITIONS

An ancient Jewish wedding feast was a huge event that often lasted a full week, even longer if the family was wealthy. Like modern weddings, the event was lavish, noisy, and expensive, but there are many significant differences between Jewish and western weddings, and these distinctions have spiritual importance.

Four phases or stages made up these ancient weddings.

1. Betrothal (Covenant)
2. Engagement period (Groom returns to his father's house, constructs an addition)
3. Groom and party arrive (Time is a surprise)
4. Marriage Feast (Celebration)

As you read through the following sequence, put on your New Testament thinking cap. Let the rich symbolism speak to your heart and inform your head on how the scarlet thread of redemption traverses both Testaments.

In the sequence of a Jewish wedding, once the man and woman agreed, an arrangement was often set by the parents. The father of the bridegroom typically negotiated a price for the bride.

Although not mentioned in the biblical narratives, Jewish tradition included a step of preparation for betrothal. The bride and groom would separately undergo a ritual immersion. The *mikvah*, or bath, was taken prior to entering into the formal betrothal period, and it was symbolic of spiritual cleansing.

Then, the bridegroom would travel to the bride's house where a legal betrothal took place. It was signified with a drink from a cup of wine. From that point on, the bride was considered set apart or sanctified for the bridegroom. The bridegroom would then leave the bride's home and return to his father's home.

Before doing so he would tell his bride to expect his return and to be prepared. The bride did not know the exact day or hour the bridegroom would return for the marriage ceremony, therefore she needed to be prepared at all times. Back home, the bridegroom would undertake the construction of a bridal chamber, adding on to his father's house.

When the father gave the word, the bridegroom and the groomsmen (Judges 14:10; John 3:28) would begin a procession to the bride's home. The bridegroom himself didn't know the exact time when this command might come.

The bride would be summoned by a shout from the street. At this time, the bridal party would travel to the father's home for a marriage feast (Matthew 25:1–6).

The bridegroom and bride went into the bridal chamber to consummate the marriage. This was followed by a seven-day marriage celebration during which time the bride remained hidden in the bridal chamber.

Finally, at the end of the seven days, the bridegroom brought his bride out for everyone to see.

The Jewish pattern in this relationship overflows into New Testament life to allow for the identification of where the church is in this sequence. In the context of the church, the bride of Christ is in the betrothal period while the Bridegroom has gone to prepare a place for His bride.

In My Father's house are many mansions; if it were not so, I would have told you. I go to prepare a place for you. And if I go and prepare a place for you, I will come again and receive you to Myself; that where I am, there you may be also. (John 14:2–3)

We are in the holy moment when Jesus expects His bride to prepare for His return. The parable of the ten virgins (Matthew 25:1–13) presents a solemn warning: Be ready. Further, the church needs to be about kingdom business.

And to her it was granted to be arrayed in fine linen, clean and bright, for the fine linen is the righteous acts of the saints. (Revelation 19:8)

How the bride conducts herself during the betrothal period will be reflected in her wedding garments.

THE FINAL CUP

Jesus came in humility the first time to work out the arrangements of the betrothal of His bride through His life, death, and resurrection from the dead. If we go back to that fateful night in the upper room in Jerusalem when Jesus took part in the Passover celebration, He projected His followers to the wedding feast, "I will not drink this wine again until that day when we are together in my Father's kingdom and the wine is new. Then I will drink it again with you" (Matthew 26:29).

What a day that will be!

SPOTLIGHT ON THE GROOM

Western wedding traditions focus on the bride. There is no question that she is the star of the show. The groom? Well, he is told to stand quietly and try not to spill anything on his tuxedo before the wedding. In fact, the start of the wedding is dependent on the bride finishing her preparations, and sometimes that leaves the groom and guests waiting.

This emphasis is the opposite of Jewish wedding priorities. Certainly, the bride is honored and celebrated, but it is the groom who is featured. The ceremony revolves around him in concert with elevating the bride.

RUNAWAY BRIDE

In 2005, a woman named Jennifer Wilbanks made national news when she created a media circus and infamously became known as the "Runaway Bride." Jennifer was scheduled to be married in Georgia in a lavish ceremony with a wedding party of twenty-eight and six hundred guests. Just days before the big event, she came down with a serious case of cold feet and disappeared, setting off a nationwide woman hunt. Three days later, she called her fiancé from a 7-Eleven in New Mexico, claiming that she had been kidnapped, assaulted, and transported west. But there was a problem—none of that was true.

The moral of the story for the church is be sure to stay faithful to the final moment. That may seem like obvious advice, but as we learned from our review of the churches in chapters two and three, just a few decades after the church was born, large segments had departed from the faith.

Jennifer was penalized with national notoriety and a felony indictment. But a faithless church will pay a much steeper price.

WHEN GOD THROWS A PARTY

The Jews had light and gladness, joy and honor. And in every province and city, wherever the king's command and decree came, the Jews had joy and gladness, a feast and a holiday. Then many of the people of the land became Jews because fear of the Jews fell upon them. (Esther 8:16–17)

Of all the many descriptions of God in the Bible, perhaps the least well-known is that of "party planner." But Scripture reveals that God is highly involved in creating and planning festivals, weddings, and parties. He enjoys throwing parties and celebrations, and He's is very good at it.

Weddings are a social highlight of modern life just as they were in ancient days. According to Knot.com, the average wedding today costs $28,000.[2]

Some cost more. Much more.

According to CBS News, "In the priciest modern-day wedding to date, this prince of Abu Dhabi had a 20,000-seat stadium specially built for his seven-day wedding to Princess Salama in 1981. This wedding fit for a king cost a whopping $100 million."[3]

If this is what earthly kings do when throwing a wedding party, just imagine what the King of Kings has in store!

THOU SHALT PARTY

Jesus did not perform His first miracle at the Temple or in a synagogue, but at a wedding feast. This was not by accident, He was making a huge statement with His choice of venue.

Consider that the Jewish calendar orbited around parties (festivals) and rest (sabbath) days that were not optional. God established seven feasts that He called "feasts of the Lord" (Leviticus 23:4). The Hebrew word for feasts means "appointed times." The timing and sequence of these events have been orchestrated by God Himself—they belong to Him.

> "Fundamentally, these seven feasts typify the sequence, timing, and significance of the major events of the Lord's redemptive career. They commence at Calvary where Jesus voluntarily gave Himself for the sins of the world (Passover), and climax at the establishment of the Kingdom at the Messiah's second coming (Tabernacles)." – Kevin Howard and Marvin Rosenthal[4]

Four of the festivals occur in the spring and were fulfilled during the ministry of Jesus.

1. Passover: Sacrifice of the Lamb
2. Feast of Unleavened Bread: The sinless Savior
3. Feast of First Fruits: Death could not hold Him
4. Pentecost: The church is born

History records the clear fulfillment of these four spring feasts through the redemptive work of Messiah. The three fall feasts will likewise be fulfilled in the future in conjunction with the second coming of Jesus.

1. Feast of Trumpets, Rosh Hashanah: a new year begins
2. Day of Atonement, Yom Kippur: when Israel repents
3. Feast of Tabernacles: when Messiah tabernacles among men

While these seven holy convocations were initially given exclusively to God's covenant nation (the Hebrew people), Jesus flung open the door of invitation to all nations.

"Then he said to his servants, 'The wedding is ready, but those who were invited were not worthy. Therefore go into the highways, and as many as you find, invite to the wedding.'" (Matthew 22:8–9)

This astonishing invitation was the crux of the chasm between Jesus and the Jewish leaders of His day. The Pharisees and Sadducees could not digest the possibility that the unclean gentiles could be welcomed into the family of God.

In fact, the blueprint to build God's family from all corners of the world should not have come as a shock to the Jewish elite leaders. The Jews were meant to be sort of spiritual bait, a cause of jealousy, luring their neighbors to desire Jehovah, the one true God.

Here are some of many Scriptures the high priest and company willfully ignored when they rejected the concept of gentile salvation.

- Israel is a light to the gentiles (Isaiah 49:6).
- All the nations will worship the Lord (Psalm 22:27).
- All the islands will wait for the law (Isaiah 42:4).
- Jacob will be a light to the gentiles, bringing salvation to

the ends of the earth (Isaiah 49:6).

- The gentiles shall come to you from the ends of the earth (Jeremiah 16:19).
- "The gentiles shall come to your light, And kings to the brightness of thy rising" (Isaiah 60:3 KJV).
- "Many nations shall be joined to the LORD in that day, and they shall become My people. And I will dwell in your midst. Then you will know that the LORD of hosts has sent Me to you" (Zechariah 2:11).

THE LORD LOVES A PARTY

Not only was the annual Jewish calendar anchored by God-ordained festivals, but each week revolved around the Sabbath, which was a time of rest, reflection, renewal, and family rejoicing. Further, the Old Testament commanded that every seven years a sabbatical year would be observed when the land of Israel was to have complete rest from cultivation for the year. To compensate for the prohibition of sowing and reaping during these twelve months, the Lord promised an extra plentiful harvest in the sixth year.

God was only warming up with the sabbath year. The year of Jubilee more fully reveals the intent of His heart—that His people should take time to enjoy Him.

The Jubilee year occurred every fiftieth year after seven sabbatical years had been celebrated. Jubilee was a radical time of restoration that interrupted the economic order of Israel. The land was to be allowed to rest (Leviticus 25:11–12). The Lord promised a triple crop to provide for the years lacking a harvest. Additionally, all hired workers and slaves were to be set free (Leviticus 25:39–54). Then, all land was to be returned to the original owner (Leviticus 25:13, 23–28).

The year of Jubilee brought Israel back to the economic structure God instituted when they were brought out of Egypt and into the promised land. Oppression was ended, ownership was restored, debts were forgiven, and slaves were freed. Jubilee looks forward to the restoring of Israel and the establishment of the messianic kingdom.

A PARTY FOR PRODIGALS

From the rest illustrated by the nap of Adam, to the gospel story of a prodigal party, to the wedding feast of the Lamb, God clearly wants His people to be consumed with resting and rejoicing. He does not want us laboring under any false burden or illusion that our works are of primary importance.

Here are some final fast facts about the protocol for the wedding party God has planned.

- You must RSVP.
- Believe in His words (John 8:30).
- It is not a potluck.
- Bring nothing but faith (Ephesians 2:8).
- Proper dress is required.
- People will be naked no more (Revelation 19:8).

FOUR ASPECTS OF THE GROOM

Chapter 19 closes out by noting four characteristics of Jesus (v. 11–21). His superior character, authority, attire, and name are all pointed out once again to make clear that no other person could ever fulfill these messianic prophecies.

There can be no mistake, Jesus Christ—Lamb, Lion, Warrior, Savior, and King—is prepared to assume His proper place.

22

JUDGMENT DAY!

Revelation 20

"Satan is like a guy in a hotel room going wild with the mini-bar. What he does not realize is that the Lord has his credit card number at the front desk, and the devil will pay." – Levi Lusko[1]

Then I saw an angel coming down from heaven, having the key to the bottomless pit and a great chain in his hand. He laid hold of the dragon, that serpent of old, who is the Devil and Satan, and bound him for a thousand years; and he cast him into the bottomless pit, and shut him up, and set a seal on him, so that he should deceive the nations no more till the thousand years were finished. But after these things he must be released for a little while. (Revelation 20:1–3)

Then why do pp resist Jesus still?

Jesus taught us to pray, "Your kingdom come, your will be done on earth as it is in heaven" (Matthew 6:10). The kingdom of God now rules over all the affairs of earth and will do so for one thousand years. In chapter 20, we find four events taking place: Satan is bound, saints reign, a final satanic rebellion occurs, and the sentencing of the condemned takes place.

SATAN IS BOUND TEMPORARILY

In (vv. 1–3) Satan is bound—it only takes one angel to apprehend the devil—a testament to the fact that the devil was never in charge! God could have taken him out at any time but allowed him to exist for His divine purpose and glory, for the salvation of souls, and for the glorification of His Son.

The phrase *bottomless pit* is mentioned 7 times in the book of Revelation; it is also called *the abyss*— the abode of demons.

Satan will be incarcerated for 1000 years. What will the world look like without Satan? The prophet Isaiah gives us an idea of what earth, and in particular Jerusalem, will be like during the millennial reign of Christ (Isaiah 11:1–10; 65:17–25).

At the end of the millennium, Satan will be released for a time. Our natural reaction might be to think that this is not the best idea. Why would God release him after one thousand years? Hasn't everyone seen enough? After the plagues, the return, one thousand years of peace, wouldn't this be enough for the world to believe in Christ and follow Him wholeheartedly?

Sadly, the answer is no. There are still some who would reject God and choose to follow the devil instead. Knowing this, God releases Satan one last time to fully rid his Kingdom of all who would seek to do the devil's bidding.

SAINTS REIGNING

The saints of God will be given governing authority with Christ on earth. John sees the souls of saints who were martyred during the Great Tribulation period, and they will also reign with Christ (v. 4b).

In verse 5, there is the phrase, "But the rest..." Who are the "rest?" They are the balance of humanity, awaiting the final judgment.

Note that those who partake of the first resurrection are called "blessed and holy." For them, the second death has no power.

Now, the second death occurs and everyone will experience a resurrection, either to eternal life or eternal condemnation (vv. 11–15).

"As the Father has life in Himself, so He has granted the Son to have life in Himself and has given Him authority to execute judgment also because He is the Son of Man. Do not marvel at this; for the hour is coming in which all who are in the graves will hear His voice and come forth — those who have done good, to the resurrection of life, and those who have done evil, to the resurrection of condemnation." (John 5:26–29)

The *resurrection of life* is the first resurrection for all those who are in Christ. The *resurrection of condemnation* is for all who have walked in wickedness and rejected Christ. This is the second death mentioned here in verse 6. Regardless, "all will hear His voice!" (Philippians 2:10–11).

Those who are of the first resurrection, the redeemed, who were judged by the world, will now judge the world during the millennial reign of Christ! Therefore, Paul declared:

Dare any of you, having a matter against another, go to law before the unrighteous, and not before the saints? Do you not know that the saints will judge the world? And if the world will be judged by you, are you unworthy to judge the smallest matters? Do you not know that we shall judge angels? How much more, things that pertain to this life? (1 Corinthians 6:1–3)

Seeing then that we will judge the world and fallen angels, let us now judge matters—socially, personally, and politically—in accordance with God's truth. Let us judge matters as priests who are in preparation of reigning with Christ. Those who are faithful with a little, God will give much!

SATANIC REBELLION

Satan is a true creature of habit with no creative genius. His tools are well-known and well-worn because of their effectiveness (2 Corinthians 2:11).

It is no surprise that the devil relapses into his old ways and starts a rebellion (vv. 7–10). God did not confine Satan to rehabilitate him, but to demonstrate His mercy toward mankind for yet another thousand years.

People will still rebel against Christ during this reign of Christ.

"For the child shall die one hundred years old,

But the sinner being one hundred years old shall be accursed." (Isaiah 65:20b)

Premature death, and even death at a moderate age (80s–90s), will be unknown. He who dies at one hundred years old shall be considered as dying in childhood or as one cut off by a curse.

Death will still be around during the millennial reign of Christ and may be used as a last-resort punishment for those who rebel against the Lord's reign. Death will not be eliminated until it is cast into hell, after the millennial reign of Christ (v. 13).

Thus, with people living a lot longer, we find in verse 8 that there is an immeasurable multitude ready to rise up in rebellion!

The reference to "Gog and Magog" does not mean the battle here is the battle of Ezekiel 38 and 39. This battle clearly occurs at the end of the millennial reign of Christ, whereas the battle in Ezekiel 38 and 39 occurs during the end times, leading up to the return of Christ. The idea here is that Satan deceives the nations once again, just as Magog was deceived by Gog (their leader) in Ezekiel 38 and 39.

In (v. 9a), the rebellious nations surround Jerusalem to destroy it. Jerusalem, during the Millennial reign of Christ, will be our Lord's capital, the center from which He reigns. But things do not go according to their evil plans (vv. 9b–10). Satan is disposed of— dispatched forever and ultimately sentenced to the lake of fire.

BIOGRAPHY OF SATAN

First appearance: Genesis 3

Job description: Job 1 and Job 2

Eviction notice:

How you are fallen from heaven,

O Lucifer, son of the morning!

How you are cut down to the ground,

You who weakened the nations!

For you have said in your heart:

"I will ascend into heaven,

I will exalt my throne above the stars of God;

I will also sit on the mount of the congregation

On the farthest sides of the north;

I will ascend above the heights of the clouds,

I will be like the Most High."

Yet you shall be brought down to Sheol,

To the lowest depths of the Pit.

Those who see you will gaze at you,

And consider you, saying:

"Is this the man who made the earth tremble,

Who shook kingdoms?" (Isaiah 14:12–16).

COMMON NAMES AND TITLES FOR SATAN

(1) Abaddon:

Hebrew name for Satan meaning "destruction" (Revelation 9:11).

(2) Accuser:

Prosecuting God's people (Revelation 12:10).

(3) Adversary:

"Be sober, be vigilant; because your adversary the devil walks about like a roaring lion, seeking whom he may devour." (1 Peter 5:8)

(4) Angel of Light:

"And no wonder! For Satan himself transforms himself into an angel of light." (2 Corinthians 11:14)

(5) Anointed Covering Cherub:

"You were the anointed cherub who covers; I established you; You were on the holy mountain of God; You walked back and forth in the midst of fiery stones." (Ezekiel 28:14)

(6) Antichrist:

"And every spirit that does not confess that Jesus Christ has come in the flesh is not of God. And this is the spirit of the Antichrist, which you have heard was coming, and is now already in the world." (1 John 4:3)

(7) Beast:

Maker of the mark (Revelation 14:10).

(8) Belial;

"And what accord has Christ with Belial? Or what part has a believer with an unbeliever?" (2 Corinthians 6:15)

(9) Deceiver:

"So the great dragon was cast out, that serpent of old, called the Devil and Satan, who deceives the whole world; he was cast to the earth, and his angels were cast out with him." (Revelation 12:9)

(10) Devil:

"He who sins is of the devil, for the devil has sinned from the beginning. For this purpose, the Son of God was manifested, that He might destroy the works of the devil." (1 John 3:8)

(11) Dragon:

"So the great dragon was cast out, that serpent of old, called the Devil and Satan, who deceives the whole world; he was cast to the earth, and his angels were cast out with him." (Revelation 12:9)

(12) Liar and Father of Lies:

"You are of your father the devil, and the desires of your father you want to do. He was a murderer from the beginning and does not stand in the truth, because there is no truth in him. When he speaks a lie, he speaks from his own resources, for he is a liar and the father of it." (John 8:44)

(13) God of this Age:

"Whose minds the god of this age has blinded, who do not believe, lest the light of the gospel of the glory of Christ, who is the image of God, should shine on them." (2 Corinthians 4:4)

(14) Lucifer:

"How you are fallen from heaven,

O Lucifer, son of the morning!" (Isaiah 14:12)

(15) Man of Sin:

False Messiah (2 Thessalonians 2:3, 4).

(16) Power of Darkness:

"He has delivered us from the power of darkness and conveyed us into the kingdom of the Son of His love, in whom we have redemption through His blood, the forgiveness of sins." (Colossians 1:13-14)

(17) Prince of the Power of the Air:

"And you He made alive, who were dead in trespasses and sins, in which you once walked according to the course of this world, *according to the prince of the power of the air, the spirit who now works in the sons of disobedience."* (Ephesians 2:1-2)

(18) Roaring Lion:

"Be sober, be vigilant; because your adversary the devil walks about like a roaring lion, seeking whom he may devour." (1 Peter 5:8)

(19) Ruler of the Darkness:

"For we do not wrestle against flesh and blood, but against principalities, against powers, against the rulers of the darkness of this age, against spiritual hosts of wickedness in the heavenly places." (Ephesians 6:12)

(20) Satan:

"And He was there in the wilderness forty days, tempted by Satan, and was with the wild beasts; and the angels ministered to Him." (Mark 1:13)

(21) Tempter:

"Now when the tempter came to Him, he said, 'If You are the Son of God, command that these stones become bread'." (Matthew 4:3)

(22) Wicked One:

"Above all, taking the shield of faith with which you will be able to quench all the fiery darts of the wicked one." (Ephesians 6:16)

ULTIMATE DEATH SENTENCE

By any name, Satan is the biggest loser of all time. He forfeited a lofty position in heaven only to end up in an eternal lake of fire (Hebrews 2:14).

Jesus confirmed this doctrine in His story regarding Lazarus (the poor man) and the rich man (Luke 16:19–31). They were in two separate places and there was a great gulf between them. Jesus was not just telling a nice story here to entertain His listeners. He was revealing what happened to the godly righteous and the godless wicked after they died. On the cross, Jesus said to the thief who believed on Him, "Today you will be with Me in paradise" (Luke 23:43).

WHAT'S NEXT?

What happens when a believer dies? Paul declared, "We are confident, yes, well pleased rather to be absent from the body and to be present with the Lord" (2 Corinthians 5:8). That's the good news in Christ.

However, the bad news is the place of the wicked dead is still open for business. Thus, its occupants are resurrected to be judged (vv. 12, 13). Scripture clearly tells us that works are not the means by which we enter heaven. The judgment of God here will determine their degree of torment in hell. Jesus rebuked Chorazin, Bethsaida, and Capernaum because they ignored His mighty works. Thus, Jesus said, "It will be more tolerable for Sodom in the day of judgment than for you!" (Matthew 11:20–24).

Believers will not appear before the great white throne judgment because our records have been abolished: "For I will forgive their iniquity, and their sin I will remember no more" (Jeremiah 31:34b). Those not found in the Book of Life have been blotted out as opposed to never being written in.

Scripture indicates people are blotted out of the Book of Life (Deuteronomy 25:6; Psalm 69:28, 109:13). The idea is that God gives everyone a chance to repent, but when people leave this world in a state of rebellion against God, He must blot out their name from the Book. God wishes for none to perish, but that all would come to repentance (2 Peter 3:9). Sadly, many church members will find themselves among those being judged at the great white throne (Matthew 7:21–23).

HELL? YES

"Then they will go away to eternal punishment, but the righteous to eternal life." (Matthew 25:46)

The harsh reality of hell is never a pleasant topic to discuss. No one spoke more clearly and frequently about hell than Jesus. It is not scripturally honest to make hell into an unpleasant myth, a fictional tool only useful for frightening rebellious children. *Hell*, by biblical definition, is a literal location that was specifically created for Satan and his horde of demons (Matthew 25:41).

FAST FACTS ABOUT HELL

(1) All mankind will exist eternally either in heaven or hell (Daniel 12:2, 3; Matthew 25:46; John 5:28; Revelation 20:14, 15).

(2) There is only one lifetime on earth to determine one's destiny (Hebrews 9:27).

(3) Eternity will be spent in either heaven or hell based on whether a person believes and puts their trust in Christ to save them (John 3:16, 36, etc.).

(4) Hell was created for Satan and his demons (Matthew 25:41; Revelation 20:10).

(5) Hell will punish the sin of those who reject Christ (Matthew 13:41, 50; Revelation 20:11–15, 21:8).

(6) Hell is conscious torment.

"and cast them into the furnace of fire. There will be wailing and gnashing of teeth" (Matthew 13:50)

"He will be tormented with fire and brimstone." (Revelation 14:10)

(7) Hell is eternal. It is final and cannot be reversed.

"The smoke of their torment goes up forever and ever and they have no rest day and night." (Revelation 14:11)

'And besides all this, between us and you there is a great gulf fixed, so that those who want to pass from here to you cannot, nor can those from there pass to us.' (Luke 16:26)

HELL: HOW CAN IT BE?

The argument is granted that the doctrine of permanent human torment in a hell populated with demons seems to be a contradiction to many of the attributes of a loving God and his eternal mercy. The problem with eliminating hell is that this results in altering the gospel, a privilege not given to any man.

Jesus gave us very clear teachings on the topic of hell. Anthony DeStefano has taken the bold step of urging everyone to take these teachings seriously in his book, *Hell: A Guide.*

DeStefano relentlessly insists that we accept hell at face value, exactly as it is portrayed in the Bible. He teaches that we must do this regardless of how offensive we find it to our human way of understanding.

First, DeStefano lays the foundation for hell by establishing the motive of its first residents, fallen angels.

"Hell exists because there are creatures there who made a permanent decision to get as far away from God as possible, no matter the consequences. Hell exists not because God wanted it, but because the rebellious angels did. In a very real sense, they invented hell, and now that they have, they have no desire to leave."[2]

Then, DeStefano touches the nerve of remorse on the part of hell's household. In his view, regret in hell does not exist.

"Do they regret this decision? Do they care that they live in hell? The short answer is no, not in the slightest. In fact, they would rather be in hell than anywhere else in creation. Not that they are happy or joyful in any way, but in a certain sense they do like being where they are, at least in terms of preferring it to the alternative: being with God in heaven. The fact that life in hell entails great suffering only adds to their resentment of God. It only adds to their prideful indignation at being victimized. It only adds fuel to their bitterness and hatred. It only makes them want to offend God more."[3]

Finally, DeStefano's guide to Hell gives alternative eternal endings no chance whatsoever. Universalism must bow to what Jesus said, without equivocation.

"The truth is that Christ couldn't have been clearer when it came to either the existence of hell or its eternal duration. When so-called theologians write books and articles that attempt to inject more 'mercy' into the words of Christ, they invariably end up going through all kinds of linguistic and intellectual gymnastics."[4]

WHAT HAPPENED TO HELL?

"At the center of the Christian tradition since the first church have been a number who insist that history is not tragic, hell is not forever, and love, in the end, wins and all will be reconciled to God." – Rob Bell[5]

No sane person enjoys entertaining thoughts of what the Bible says about hell. To resolve this terrific tension, many schools of thought have developed to soften or even remove Scripture's insistence of the permanent plight of souls. Scripture is clear that people without Christ are plunged into a very real place of unimaginable torment, no matter how much mankind might wish it weren't so.

Just like the joys of heaven seem too good to be true, the horrors of hell seem too bad to be true. Almost. Remarkably, some have dealt with this—the ultimate of sober and gravely serious subjects—by employing whimsy or arrogant disdain.

Ted Turner famously commented, "I'd rather go to hell. Heaven has got to be boring."[6]

Or as Woody Allen said, "Hell is Manhattan at rush hour. There's no question there is an unseen world. The question is, how far is it from midtown and how late does it stay open."[7]

Rob Bell is only the latest in a long line of apologists who bend the Bible to accomplish their goals. Annihilationism, soul-sleep, second chance theology and universalism are a few of the paths presented to avoid the harsh realities of hell. The glaring Achilles heel of each is the fundamental immortality of the human soul coupled with the certainty of man's responsibility for his sin.

"Hell exists, but no one is in it." – *Richard Neuhaus.*[8]

Compare those words with these of Jonathan Edwards.

"O sinner! Consider the fearful danger you are in: it is a great furnace of wrath, a wide and bottomless pit, full of the fire of wrath, that you are held over in the hand of that God, whose wrath is provoked and incensed as much against you, as against many of the damned in hell. You hang by a slender thread, with the flames of divine wrath flashing about it, and ready every moment to singe it, and burn it asunder; and you have no interest in any Mediator, and nothing to lay hold of to save yourself, nothing to keep off the flames of wrath, nothing of your own, nothing that you ever have done, nothing that you can do, to induce God to spare you one moment." – Jonathan Edwards[9]

Without apology, Edwards simply echoes what Scripture speaks for itself.

The devil, who deceived them, was cast into the lake of fire and brimstone where the beast and the false prophet are. And they will be tormented day and night forever and ever. ... The sea gave up the dead who were in it, and Death and Hades delivered up the dead who were in them. And they were judged, each one according to his works. ... And anyone not found written in the Book of Life was cast into the lake of fire. (Revelation 20:10, 13, 15)

Let there be no doubt—those that would dilute the clear warnings of the terror of an eternity in hell are doing no favors to their hearers. In fact, they are doing a severe disservice to the burden of faithful messengers. The ambassador code of honor demands a pure transmission of the message they are entrusted with. Altering its contents is a betrayal and a travesty.

When the apostle Paul rested his head on the executioner's block in Rome, his legacy was secure in the confidence that he had declared the full counsel of God's word without edit (Acts 20:27).

As John MacArthur said, "Satan continues his efforts to make sin less offensive, heaven less appealing, hell less horrific and the gospel less urgent."[10]

Any effort to deny that hell has permanent irredeemable human residents is in fact a detraction to the unique work Jesus was required to perform on the cross. His pleading to His Father, "*If* [emphasis added] there be another way...*" received no reply (Matthew 26:39).

It is no small matter to detract from the seriousness of the bad side of the good news. Suggesting that God will issue full pardon to those who reject Him is a serious offense. Scripture forbids diminishing the full impact of any part of God's Word.

And if anyone takes away from the words of the book of this prophecy, God shall take away his part from the Book of Life, from the holy city, and from the things which are written in this book. (Revelation 22:19)

Edwards understood this stark admonition, and it led him to a crystal-clear declaration.

"Thus it will be with you that are in an unconverted state, if you continue in it; the infinite might, and majesty, and terribleness of the omnipotent God shall be magnified upon you, in the ineffable strength of your torments. You shall be tormented in the presence of the holy angels, and in the presence of the Lamb; and when you shall be in this state of suffering, the glorious inhabitants of heaven shall go forth and look on the awful spectacle, that they may see what the wrath and fierceness of the Almighty is; and when they have seen it, they will fall down and adore that great power and majesty ... Oh sinner, consider what terrible danger you are in." - Jonathan Edwards[11]

DANTE'S INFERNO

"Through me you pass into the city of woe. Through me you pass into eternal pain. All hope abandon, ye who enter here." – Dante Alighieri[12]

All major religions contain a variation on the theme of punishment after death for sins committed in this life.

C.S. Lewis wrote, "There are only two kinds of people in the end: those who say to God, 'Thy will be done' and those to whom God says, in the end, 'Thy will be done.' All that are in hell choose it."[13]

Fully grasping the enormity of this truth is beyond human capacity, but we have been told enough, and to whom much is given, much is required (Luke 12:48).

The classic English preacher Charles Spurgeon understood this principle well, and while he took no joy in its declaration, he allowed no misguided human emotion or fantasy to color his message.

"There is a real fire in hell, as truly as you have a real body, a fire exactly like that which we have on this earth except this; that it will not consume though it will torture you. You have seen asbestos lying amid hot coals, but not consumed. So your body will be prepared by God in such a way that it will burn forever without being desensitized for all its raging fury." – Charles Spurgeon[14]

In any court of law, firsthand witnesses are always judged to have primary evidentiary weight. In fact, 'hearsay' evidence is often excluded. So when it comes to the heavy matters of heaven, hell, eternity, paradise, and punishment, who should be believed?

Only one person in history has been to both heaven and hell and brought a report back to earth. Many other opinions have been proclaimed and published throughout history. Where will you place your trust? John Lennon? John Stott? Rob Bell? Or Jesus Christ? The answer should be obvious. Unfortunately, that is frequently not the case.

Be very careful who you listen to, and pay even closer attention who you follow into the grave.

"If your hand causes you to sin, cut it off. It is better for you to enter into life maimed, rather than having two hands, to go to hell, into the fire that shall never be quenched." (Mark 9:43)

One of the Seven Wonders of the World is the famous structure of the Taj Mahal, built as a monument of love in the mid-1600s. Twenty-eight types of jewels are embedded in the palace marble. For 22 years, 20,000 workers labored to build this masterpiece with the help of 1,000 elephants. It comes as a surprise to many visitors to India to discover that this lavish monument was not a palace at all but rather a tomb, built by a wealthy shah for his beloved wife.

If one Indian husband could plan and construct the breathtakingly beautiful Taj Mahal for a woman to whom he was married for only fourteen years, what could God be preparing as a home where we will live forever with Him?

A TERRIBLE PARABLE: LAZARUS AND THE RICH MAN

In this chilling story recorded in Luke 16:19–31, Jesus pulled the curtain back between this life and the next. Lazarus lived a life of deprivation while the unnamed rich man enjoyed his luxuries. At death, the tables were turned, and the lessons unfold.

YOUR WORST PROBLEM

Principles we learn from Luke 16:19–31:

- Death is inevitable for all.
- There is a final judgment.
- All will give an account for the things done in the body.
- There are memories in hell.
- There is awareness of heaven.
- A great gulf is fixed between heaven and hell.

GOD'S ONLY SOLUTION: JESUS

In response to man's predicament, God sent a savior, His son Jesus.

- God so loved the world that He sent Jesus.
- Jesus provided exclusive salvation. No one comes to the Father otherwise.
- Anyone and everyone, whosoever will, may come to Him for forgiveness.
- Today is the day for salvation.

TWO DESTINATIONS, NO SUBSTITUTIONS

Here are some of the various biblical terms for two dramatically different destinations for life after death.

- *Sheol* is a Hebrew term describing the grave and death.
- *Hades* is a Greek word that often points to hell, a place of torment (Luke 10:15).
- *Gehenna* is a Greek word, taken from a literal burning garbage dump southeast of Jerusalem, referring to hell as a place of torment (Matthew 5:30, 23:33).
- The lake of fire is the final place after their resurrection for those who do not believe (Revelation 20:14–15).
- Paradise is a place of comfort and joy (Luke 23:43).
- The new heavens and the new earth are where believers will live after their resurrection (Revelation 20:4–6).
- Paradise is a place of eternal comfort (Revelation 23:42).

A STUNNING SURPRISE

The Bible teaches that there will be two resurrections, one for the saved and one for the unsaved.

Not even the most vivid imagination can project the first moment after death for those who have placed their trust in Jesus Christ in this life. Paradise will include the firm rule of Jesus, removal of all collateral damage caused by the curse, harmony with animals, and, finally world peace.

The millennial rule of Christ will display all the spectacular promises of the Bible in full bloom. Holiness will take on a new reality as it pervades every aspect of life in the kingdom. All traces of evil, profanity, and sinful tendencies will vanish. The original blueprint of God in the garden will come back into view.

A RUDE AWAKENING

The great white throne judgment (Revelation 20:11–15) represents the purity, holiness, and power of the One who sits on the throne, capable and worthy of proclaiming final judgment.

The Bible forbids man to pass final judgment on any fellow human being (Luke 6:37). This passage is often misunderstood and misused. Jesus was not referring to temporal issues of moral and immoral behavior but was prohibiting the issuing of final edicts of condemnation and final judgment. This awesome privilege is reserved for God alone.

Men come to conclusions based on faulty and incomplete information. Not only does God know all the facts, He knows all the motives of the heart. Vengeance and judgment belong only to the Lord. No one else could bear the weight of knowing what lies ahead for the unforgiven sinner.

"After Jesus finishes judging the unsaved, they will be condemned to this place called the lake of fire. They will remain there for all eternity. Their pain and torment will never cease." – Jeff Lasseigne[15]

UNIMAGINABLE

Jesus said that some will be thrown outside into the darkness, where there will be weeping and gnashing of teeth (Matthew 8:12). This led one commentator to say:

"In hell, people are not merely there in spirit, but in bodily form. Their senses are greatly increased, there is a foul odor, screams, the heat is unbearable, the people are always thirsty, always hungry, their desires (sex, drugs, etc.) are multiplied and never fulfilled, there is a pervading fear, you have no strength, no rest nor sleep, no mercy, no water, no life, you are naked, you do not have time to get lost in your thoughts, and there is no purpose—all is over, lost, gone." – Author unknown

Jesus was clear and firm about the terms of hell: it is final and eternal.

WHAT IS TRUE

Everyone has enough light to find God. What about the remote tribes who never hear the gospel? They have their conscience and creation to illuminate their need for God (Romans 1:20, 2:15). If they respond to the light they have, God will illumine a path that will lead to Him.

WHAT IS FALSE

- Purgatory
- Reincarnation
- Spiritism (communicating with the dead)
- Universalism (all will be saved)
- Annihilationism (there is no awareness after death)

THERE WILL BE PRAYERS IN HELL

You may not have time to pray now, but some will find plenty of time to pray in eternity as the rich man did (Luke 16:27).

But the response will be the most stinging, most crushing, most regret-inducing words ever uttered: "Too late."

23

A GLIMPSE OF ETERNAL GLORY

Revelation 21

"If sinners be damned, at least let them leap to hell over our bodies. If they will perish, let them perish with our arms about their knees. Let no one go there unwarned and unprayed for." – Charles Spurgeon[1]

Now I saw a new heaven and a new earth, for the first heaven and the first earth had passed away. Also, there was no more sea. (Revelation 21:1)

We are moving towards the conclusion of this glorious book of Revelation.

Following the one-thousand-year reign of Christ, we see Satan's banishment to an eternal hell, and the great white throne judgment. The new heaven and earth now appear.

What we behold here will come to pass because God is faithful and true. This is the irrevocable, eternal destiny of all those in Christ (vv. 1–4).

The former things, all the temporal things of the old earth, all the things people lie, cheat, steal, and sell their souls to possess, are gone! A new heaven and earth have replaced the old.

The heaven mentioned here is not the realm where God the Father dwells. It is not the celestial domain, meaning our planetary or stellar heavens. Rather, this is the atmosphere, the sky surrounding the earth. Right now, this is the territory of the devil (Ephesians 2:1, 2) as he is the prince of the power of the air.

Peter gives us insight as to how the old earth and heaven will pass away (2 Peter 3:10–13). *Dissolved* means literally "to loosen, break up, and melt." Despite the hysteria of many today, the earth will not be destroyed by mankind, but by God Himself.

Scripture tells us that it is God who renews (keeps) the earth (Psalm 104:30). Jesus, not our environmental programs, is literally holding this world together.

What is meant by the reference in verse 1 to no more sea? This doesn't mean there will be no more water. Rather, it points to a new geographical arrangement of waters on the new earth, possibly to provide more land for its inhabitants.

John saw the new Jerusalem descending from heaven, the abode of God (v. 2). This congregation is adorned as a bride, for the bride is the church!

The new temple represents the fact that God has come to the tabernacle. That is, He abides with His creation. This was the original intent in the garden of Eden. He not only wipes away every tear, He removes the cause for every tear. There will be no more death, sorrow, crying, or pain (Isaiah 65:17). All things are made new. When God says something is finished, it is finished. There is nothing we can add or take away from His work. All that remains is for mankind to enjoy Him forevermore.

HEAVEN IS A WONDERFUL PLACE

"Phillip of Macedon, father of Alexander the Great, commissioned a servant to stand in his presence each day and say, 'Phillip, you will die.' In contrast, France's Louis XIV decreed that the word death not be uttered in his presence. Most of us are more like Louis than Phillip, denying death and avoiding the thought of it except when it's forced upon us. We live under the fear of death." – Randy Alcorn[2]

"And God will wipe away every tear from their eyes; there shall be no more death, nor sorrow, nor crying. There shall be no more pain, for the former things have passed away." (Revelation 21:4)

Are you looking forward to heaven? For Christians, that should be a rhetorical question with an automatic answer. But that is often not the case.

We need to talk more about heaven. Unfortunately, misinformation about heaven has gained wide acceptance and caused the church to surrender one of the strongest benefits of the faith. No other religion, no philosophy, and no medical treatment can offer the guarantee, the certainty, of life after death.

The demands and details of daily life can obscure the most fundamental question of life: What will happen when you die? Nineteenth-century British theologian J.C. Ryle said, "I pity the man who never thinks about heaven."[3]

As Paul observed, "If in this life only we have hope in Christ, we are of all men the most pitiable" (1 Corinthians 15:19).

What would cause even serious, sincere Christians to neglect this crucial hope?

UNBIBLICAL VIEWS OF HEAVEN

Even well-known and respected theologians have sometimes skirted the issue of heaven. Some leaders have even discouraged the study of the book of Revelation because "it is a sealed book." That will come as breaking news to the apostle John because there is an inherent promise of blessing simply for reading this book.

Blessed is he who reads and those who hear the words of this prophecy, and keep those things which are written in it; for the time is near. (Revelation 1:3)

Further, the very title *Revelation* comes from the Greek word *apokálypsis*, which means "the unveiling"—quite the opposite of closed and sealed!

Think of the presentation of a statue at an art museum. The new work is covered by a tarp and, at the right moment, it is unveiled for all to see. That is the picture of the theme of this book.

Misinformation about the destiny of the church has a number of propaganda outlets but only one source: the father of lies. As we read about the beast in Revelation 13:6.

"Then he opened his mouth in blasphemy against God, to blaspheme His name, His tabernacle, and those who dwell in heaven."

Notice, Satan is not content to slander God and those in heaven, but he speaks evil about heaven itself. Not surprisingly, he was evicted from this place (Isaiah 14:12–15). Satan became embittered not only to God but also to His dwelling place. As it is said, "misery loves company." Since he can no longer enjoy access to the privilege of heaven, the devil wants no one to set their hearts on this magnificent future.

A WORLD WITHOUT YOU

It is difficult for our minds to grasp the fact that the world existed before our birth and it will continue spinning after we are dead. This harsh truth needs to be translated to living a life now that invests in and prepares for life after death. Amos wisely warned, "Prepare to meet your God" (Amos 4:12). We should consider this brief life as a staging ground, a time of preparation for the next.

Yes, the world will continue when you have departed, but you can leave behind a legacy saturated with determination to invest in eternity. You can make the maximum impact for Christ during your time on earth.

SIX WORDS CHANGE EVERYTHING

There will be no more curse. (Revelation 22:3a)

That is a phenomenal promise. When you couple it with the words of Revelation 22:1, that there will be a new earth, well folks, we have a whole new ballgame. All the negatives of the fall are erased while unimaginable pleasures replace them. What is not to like? Why wouldn't the whole world stand in line to accept God's terms for life eternal in heaven?

A clue to the answer is found in the parable of the rich man and Lazarus, (Luke 16:20–35). It is revealing that the wealthy man only asks for relief from his suffering. He does not ask for entrance into heaven.

You see, the glories of heaven are obviously attractive in comparison to the alternative, but that is not the full story. What is the central activity of heaven? Worshiping God! Could it be that this is what causes them to reject the gospel?

People who are repulsed by humbly submitting to God in this life will have no interest in doing so forever. Sad but true. Even when all hell is breaking loose on earth, the self-destructive, fallen nature of man will demand its own suicidal path—even to the very last moment.

DARK DAYS BUT A BRIGHT FUTURE

Every experience you have ever had was tinged by your fallen nature. Each thought, action, and plan has been filtered through a mind that has been altered by sin, and you are far from alone in this.

For we know that the whole creation groans and labors with birth pangs together until now. (Romans 8:22)

Everyone and everything on earth since the garden of Eden has been subject to the bondage of corruption. Glimmers of earthly glory inspired Louis Armstrong to sing, "What a Wonderful World." There are wonderful things in this world, and we can wax optimistic. But then the sun comes up, and we see the brutal reality of a rebel race living on a poisoned planet where hope is extinguished by the reality of suffering and death. This subjection to futility would become the inspiration for Peggy Lee's melancholy song, "Is That All There Is?"

Thank God that this gloom and doom do not have the final word. Far from it.

For I consider that the sufferings of this present time are not worthy to be compared with the glory which shall be revealed in us. For the earnest expectation of the creation eagerly waits for the revealing of the sons of God. (Romans 8:18–19)

In all creation, we can see the hope and anticipation that sin and death will reach their expiration date. Yes, a truly wonderful world is on the way.

As long as we are using songs to illustrate these truths, let's remember this one, "I Can Only Imagine."

"I can only imagine when that day comes

When I find myself standing in the Son

I can only imagine when all I would do is forever

Forever worship You

I can only imagine

I can only imagine"[4]

The hollow longing that human hearts feel is due to the fact that nothing on earth can truly satisfy us. This longing is an echo of the fact that God has placed eternity in each heart. We know something is missing. Until each restless soul finds the safe harbor of God's grace and forgiveness, they will wander about in a gray twilight zone, uncomfortable with the present and unsure of the future.

For the hearts of this people have grown dull.

Their ears are hard of hearing,

And their eyes they have closed,

Lest they should see with their eyes and hear with their ears,

Lest they should understand with their hearts and turn,

So that I should heal them. (Matthew 13:15)

Here are more words about heaven from Randy Alcorn:

"To long for Christ is to long for heaven, for that is where we will be with Him. God's people are 'longing for a better country' (Hebrews 11:16). We cannot set our eyes on Christ without setting our eyes on heaven and we cannot set our eyes on heaven without setting our eyes on Christ." – Randy Alcorn[5]

(ALMOST) TOO GOOD TO BE TRUE

Have you ever booked a hotel based on its website, and then you were deeply disappointed at check-in? A wide-angle lens made the rooms look huge and clean, the pool appeared to be massive and open, and the pictures were not taken in this century. This is a classic case of false advertising.

Heaven has the opposite problem because words cannot adequately describe how fantastic it is and how long we will have to enjoy it. Our problem here is that deep inside we know we do not belong there. Relax friends; that is precisely what grace is all about.

This is why Jesus said, "Do not fear, little flock, for it is your Father's good pleasure to give you the kingdom" (Luke 12:32). The book of Revelation is the closest thing we have to a website for heaven. If someone were to make a summary presentation, here are some of the bullet points they might use:

FAST FACTS ABOUT HEAVEN

- God is there (Revelation 21:22–27). If that was the only feature of heaven, we could say, "*dayenu*," which is Hebrew for "more than enough."
- There are saved people from every tribe and nation. The total is in the billions, making for a lot of new friends!
- There are new types of friends too. Zillions of angels will be there (Revelation 5:11). The Bible says "myriads of myriads," but this word, zillions, also works.
- No more curse, tears, death, pain, grief, regret, depression, abortions, addiction, abuse, fear, crime, pornography, drugs, hospitals, funerals, dentists, commercials, taxes, or anything even slightly unpleasant (Revelation 7:15–17).
- There will be a new and improved earth (Revelation 21).
- Imagine everything evil removed and everything good multiplied by infinity. That is your first moment in heaven. Buckle up.
- There will be room to roam (Revelation 21:16–17).
- The new Jerusalem alone will be 1,500 square miles, about the size of Montana, but it will also have the same vertical dimension.
- We will return back to the garden (Revelation 22:2).
- The angel with a flaming sword guarding the gate to

Eden since the fall will be reassigned because the Tree of
Life will be available to all in the new Jerusalem.

IDOLATERS, OVERCOMERS, AND THE NEW JERUSALEM

Through faith in Christ, we are overcomers (1 John 5:5). The
cowardly, timid, and faithless are all called out (v. 8), along with
this infamous list:

- Unbelievers
- Untrustworthy people
- Detestable idolaters (the worship of images)
- Murderers
- Sexually immoral people
- Sorcerers—one who relies upon drugs and 'magical'
  remedies, which poison the mind
- Liars

The good news is that Christ died for every one of these sins (1
Corinthians 6:9–11). Only His blood can wash away the guilty
stains of our sins. In verse 9, we see the bride, the inhabitants of
the new Jerusalem. In verses 10 through 21, John describes the
new Jerusalem adorned as a bride in splendor and beauty.

This is not another new Jerusalem, but rather a continuation of
John's description of the city, which he started in verse 2.

The measurements here are literal, according to the measure of a
man. One furlong (v.16) is about 660 feet; the total calculation
results in 1,500 miles squared. That's how large the new
Jerusalem will be! The new Jerusalem will literally come down
out of heaven. Its walls are a clear greenish crystal (v. 11),
measuring one hundred forty-four cubits or 216 feet (see
tourofheaven.com for more descriptions of heaven).

In verses 19 to 21, John describes the twelve foundations, the gates, and the streets of the city. From bottom to the top:

1. Jasper (a clear greenish crystal)
2. Sapphire (a blue stone)
3. Chalcedony (a greenish-blue stone)
4. Emerald (a green stone)
5. Sardonyx (bluish-white stone streaked with brown or red)
6. Sardius (a red stone)
7. Chrysolite (a yellow quartz stone)
8. Beryl (a yellow-green stone)
9. Topaz (a natural golden-brown or yellow stone)
10. Chrysoprase (a golden-green stone)
11. Jacinth (an orange-brown stone)
12. Amethyst (a violet or purple stone)

What a glorious scene: gates of precious stones and streets of gold (v. 21), no temple, sun, or night will be there (vv. 22–27), and all the nations, *ethnos* (ethnicities), will enter the city with all reverence.

BUT WAIT, THERE'S MORE

"It is also interesting that the Hebrew sage known as Nachmonides, writing in the 13th century, concluded from his study of the Book of Genesis that the universe has ten dimensions, but only four of them are "knowable" by man. It appears that many millions of dollars have been spent on atomic accelerators only to learn what Nachmonides concluded from his study of the text of Genesis! From hints in Paul's Epistle to the Romans, some of us suspect that the original creation was 'fractured' as a result of the curse declared in Genesis 3." – Chuck Missler[6]

Dogs have much more sensitive ears than humans, hearing sounds up to four times farther away. "They have up to 300 million olfactory receptors in their noses, versus only about 6 million for us. And the part of their brain dedicated to interpreting these is about 40 times larger than ours," according to Michael T. Nappier, DVM, DABVP, of the Virginia Maryland College of Veterinary Medicine.[7]

By some estimates, there are animals that can see about 100 million different colors or about 99 million more than we can! This is due largely to the fact that many tetrachromats have a fourth cone sensitive to the ultraviolet part of the spectrum, which is invisible to the human.

These mind-bending facts surely whet our appetites to know more about our future bodies and our future home. But as we are about to learn, much of the information about heaven is beyond our capability to process, understand, and receive—it's more than we could bear.

WHAT GOD CAN'T TELL YOU

Of all the documents that have ever existed on earth, the book of Revelation has the deepest and most reliable information about heaven. Still, this dazzling book can remain somewhat frustrating. For all its illumination, Revelation contains startling scenes, puzzling symbols, and controversial information which creates as many questions as it answers.

This is not a complaint but rather an observation. We need to be grateful for the information God has chosen to bless us with. Perhaps we should view Revelation as a super movie trailer, an extended preview of coming attractions. The fact is that there are things God cannot tell us for a variety of reasons, and sometimes words simply fail.

Jesus put it this way to Nicodemus, a learned teacher of Israel, "If I have told you earthly things and you do not believe, how will you believe if I tell you heavenly things?" (John 3:12).

Our earthly minds have limitations that inhibit us from completely absorbing heavenly truths. Therefore, the Bible is chock full of symbols, parables, and relational teachings. A common phrase is "The kingdom of heaven is like..." (see Matthew 13:24, for one example among many).

A fascinating story shared by the apostle Paul sheds some light on human limits.

I know a man in Christ who fourteen years ago—whether in the body I do not know, or whether out of the body I do not know, God knows—such a one was caught up to the third heaven. And I know such a man—whether in the body or out of the body I do not know, God knows—how he was caught up into Paradise and heard inexpressible words, which it is not lawful for a man to utter. (2 Corinthian 12:2–4)

Note the use of the terms "inexpressible" and "not lawful" (v. 4). The first tells us that the container of language simply will not hold heavenly truth. The second actually says that what was seen in paradise is too sacred to be communicated on earth. From these statements, we realize that stuffing heavenly truth into earthly language is not only clumsy but also sometimes impossible, since no terms of speech are fit to express such sublime ideas.

Psalm 103 provides interesting insight and confirms that access to God's nature can be determined by the level of our relationship with the Lord.

He made known His ways to Moses, His acts to the children of Israel. (Psalm 103:7)

Some are spectators to the works of God, but others draw close and come to understand His very nature. Further, spiritual deafness can be self-induced when we fail to grow into maturity.

Of whom we have much to say, and hard to explain, since you have become dull of hearing. (Hebrews 5:11)

True, in this life, we cannot know everything about God's kingdom, but let's be certain to take full advantage of the revelation we do have. Our God is the Alpha and Omega (the first and last letters of the Hebrew alphabet), the beginning and the end; Jesus declared Himself to be the same (1:8; 22:13).

"Our Savior kneels down and gazes upon the darkest acts of our lives. But rather than recoil in horror, he reaches out in kindness and says, "I can clean that if you want." And from the basin of his grace, he scoops a palm-full of mercy and washes away our sin." — Max Lucado[8]

24

ALTERNATIVE ENDINGS

"You cannot go back and change your beginning, but you can start from here and change your ending."- C.S. Lewis[1]

When some Hollywood films are produced, they are filmed with several different endings. Some are screened by focus groups and others by studio executives. Their goal is to predict which will be more attractive to movie audiences.

Imagine *Titanic* where Jack lives, or a *Rambo I* that ends with John committing suicide. Alternative endings.

Today, there are still alternative endings for your life.

Your destiny is not fixed in the stars, determined by your DNA, or picked by your parents. You choose where you will spend eternity. You cannot change the fact that you will be alive and aware forever, but you do pick the place where you will spend your existence after this life ends. The best-known Scripture states this fact plainly:

"For God so loved the world that He gave His only begotten Son, that whoever believes in Him should not perish but have everlasting life." (John 3:16)

Simply, John 3:16 revolves around the profound truth that your decision to believe in Jesus, or not to believe in Jesus, will decide your destiny.

CHOOSE YOUR ENDING

There are many things you cannot control about your life, such as where and when you were born or your family. All dictate many directions your life has taken. But nobody except you can decide how you will spend the afterlife.

Two questions should be carefully considered by everyone: Where will you be one second after you die? And how will you be rewarded in eternity?

Every temporal issue is trivial in comparison to these colossal questions. The most common error about the next life is not blatant false doctrine but simple neglect. Most people simply don't want to face and deal with the reality that these bodies will inevitably betray us—then what?

The worst strategy ever is to exhibit indifference towards the topic and decide, "We can't know for sure, so I will just wait and see what happens." That will be too late.

Randy Alcorn asks, "When you leave this world, will you be known as one who accumulated treasures on earth that you couldn't keep? Or will you be recognized as one who invested treasures in heaven that you couldn't lose?"[2]

As Peter wrote, "Therefore, since all these things will be dissolved, what manner of persons ought you to be in holy conduct and godliness?" (2 Peter 3:11). The answer is obvious. Charles Spurgeon weighed in with this statement of fact, "It is a fool who does not spend this life preparing for the next."

YOUR BEST DAY, THE WORST DAY

For the person who is forgiven and confident in their salvation, a place in paradise is assured. This will be your best day. But full disclosure is mandated because there is another awful option: if a soul enters eternity still carrying unforgiven sin, this will be their worst day.

Jesus said to the unrepentant, "Depart from Me, you cursed, into the everlasting fire prepared for the devil and his angels" (Matthew 25:41). You do not want to hear those words and you do not have to. But to be crystal clear, it is up to you.

MASTERPIECE RESTORATION

Everyone knows Leonardo da Vinci's most famous painting, the *Mona Lisa*. One of his lesser-known works is titled *Salvator Mundi*—Savior of the World. This was painted by da Vinci around 1500 for King Louis XII of France.

Lost for over 200 years, *Salvator Mundi* fell into the hands of amateurs who "touched up" this masterpiece, varnished it, and even dared to paint over some areas. The painting surfaced in early 1958 in London where it sold at auction for 45 British pounds ($125).

In 2007, the painting was found by expert art restorers in New York who undertook 6 years of meticulous restoration.

The result? In 2017, it sold for $450.3 million at Christie's, the most ever paid to date for a piece of art.

YOU ARE THE MASTERPIECE

Do you see the parallels between the *Salvator Mundi* story and your life?

You too were created by a genius, and you are His masterpiece, the very crown of creation. Like the *Salvator Mundi*, you were lost. Your soul was covered by the grime of this world and your beauty was obscured by layers of varnish.

Ruined by sin, undervalued, and sold cheap, you were without power to return to your original glory and achieve what you were meant to be.

That's where a savior comes in. While da Vinci's work was rescued by a team of experts, only Jesus, the solitary Savior, can save you.

Finally, the salvaged painting was redeemed for millions. Your soul was bought with far more than a King's ransom. It was paid for with the life of Jesus.

NOW WHAT?

Those who are wise shall shine

Like the brightness of the firmament,

And those who turn many to righteousness

Like the stars forever and ever. (Daniel 12:3)

Bob Goff said, "I used to be afraid of failing at something that really mattered to me, but now I'm more afraid of succeeding at things that don't matter."[3]

When Jesus chose His words to describe the divide between the old, unredeemed life and a forgiven one, He chose the most powerful phrase imaginable. "You must," Jesus said, "be born again" (John 3:7b).

Once you have asked God to forgive you in Jesus' name, you have made the most important decision. You are forgiven, your sins forgotten by God, and the narrow path to heaven lies before you.

How you chose to spend your life between this breath and your last one will contribute to how you are rewarded in eternity. Yes, there is a baseline of reward guaranteed by salvation. Beyond that, there are alternative endings available to you.

WORST STOCK TRADE EVER

What are you investing in? I am not talking about 401ks and retirement funds but real treasure: your time, energy, and passion. It is possible to have a saved soul but live a lost life.

But others save with fear, pulling them out of the fire, hating even the garment defiled by the flesh. (Jude v. 23)

Let's illustrate with the story of perhaps the worst stock trade ever.

In April 1976, Ronald Wayne was a co-founder and 10-percent shareholder of Apple Computer. He wrote manuals and designed the early Apple logo. He was on the ground floor of a massive revolution.

But he was uncomfortable with some of the unorthodox ways of Steve Jobs, who refused to do test marketing on his products. So

Ronald sold his stock for $800. Since then Apple, as you might know, has done okay.

Had Wayne held on to his shares, that 10-percent stake would today be worth over $192 billion dollars.[4]

Did you gasp? Don't. A Christian who voluntarily forfeits their brief, shining time on earth for paltry pleasures instead of serving, sacrificing, and being about the Father's business is squandering far more than Ronald Wayne ever did.

DESTINED FOR THE THRONE

"The church and only the church is the key to and explanation of history. The church, blood-washed and spotless is the goal of all of God's vast creative handiwork. Therefore history is only the handmaiden of the church. Nations are only puppets, manipulated by God for the purposes of His church. Creation has no other name, history has no other goal...From the foundation of the earth to the eternal ages, God has been working towards one grand event, one supreme end—the glorious wedding of His Son, the Marriage Supper of the Lamb." – Paul Billheimer[5]

Nothing in this life is more important than living now, so you will hear these words then:

"His lord said to him, 'Well done, good and faithful servant; you were faithful over a few things, I will make you ruler over many things. Enter into the joy of your lord.'" (Matthew 25:21)

Consider yourself the scriptwriter for the drama that is your life. How is it going to end? In triumph, or with the tragic loss of rewards?

Now if anyone builds on this foundation with gold, silver, precious stones, wood, hay, straw, each one's work will become clear; for the Day will declare it, because it will be revealed by fire; and the fire will test each one's work, of what sort it is. If anyone's work which he has built on it endures, he will receive a reward. If anyone's work is burned, he will suffer loss; but he himself will be saved, yet so as through fire. (1 Corinthians 3:12 – 15)

25

PREPARE TO MEET THY GOD

"We are such half-hearted creatures, middling about with drink and sex and ambition when infinite joy is offered us." – C.S. Lewis[1]

Who is the most famous celebrity you have ever met? Perhaps a film star, an athlete, or a politician? It is interesting how people react when a big personality walks into a restaurant. Some try to be cool and pretend nothing has happened. Others point, shoot selfies, and act giddy. Of course someone is always going to slide in for an autograph.

While we all have different celebrity experiences in our past, I can tell you the most important person you will meet in your future: Jesus!

When we discuss the perfect atmosphere of the next life, it is easy to get caught up in the spectacular scenery, the amazing inhabitants, and all the new senses we will be experiencing. There will be six-winged angels flying about, other beings chanting "Holy, Holy, Holy," and 24 elders on thrones worshiping God. Combine this with an emerald rainbow, a crystal sea, the shekinah glory, and above all, meeting Him personally. What a moment that will be!

Let's assume your interview will take place at the reward (behma) seat of Christ (2 Corinthians 5:10), rather than the great white throne. In either case, everyone will have their moment.

SAVE THE DATE

For we must all appear before the judgment seat of Christ, that each one may receive the things done in the body, according to what he has done, whether good or bad. (2 Corinthians 5:10)

We have all become accustomed to receiving event invitations that encourage us to "save the date." Sometimes these come without full information. They are tentative—pending further communication—but we put it on our calendar anyway. That is the principle behind preparing to meet God.

We do not yet have all the details about when and how, but we absolutely know the day is approaching. Without fail, we will all see God face to face someday. It is simply a matter of time.

George Müller said of our entrance into heaven, "We should be like vessels in full sail entering the port, having an abundant entrance. Let us aim after this, calmly and quietly bidding adieu to this evil world, joyously waiting for the coming of the Lord, rejoicing in the Lord abundantly."[2]

PEOPLE GET READY

"His lord said to him, 'Well done, good and faithful servant; you were faithful over a few things, I will make you ruler over many things. Enter into the joy of your lord.'" (Matthew 25:21)

"God comes right out and tells us why he gives us more money than we need. It's not so we can find more ways to spend it. It's not so we can indulge ourselves and spoil our children. It's not so we can insulate ourselves from needing God's provision. It's so we can give and give generously." – Randy Alcorn[3]

That leads us to the lightning round. It's time to lay out the calls to action that will properly prepare us for eternity:

But lay up for yourselves treasures in heaven, where neither moth nor rust doth corrupt, and where thieves do not break through nor steal. (Matthew 6:20 KJV)

For whosoever shall give you a cup of water to drink in my name, because ye belong to Christ, verily I say unto you, he shall not lose his reward. (Mark 9:41 KJV)

And the King shall answer and say unto them, Verily I say unto you, Inasmuch as ye have done it unto one of the least of these my brethren, ye have done it unto me. (Matthew 25:40 KJV)

Let's land on the powerful points of the parable of the talents.

And unto one he gave five talents, to another two, and to another one; to every man according to his several abilities; and straightway took his journey. (Matthew 25:15 KJV)

From this parable, we see that everyone has something to offer, and they will be evaluated based on their faithfulness, not their fruitfulness. Remember, Noah and Jeremiah had little success from a numerical standpoint. And yet we can be sure they were warmly welcomed and rewarded upon their entry into heaven.

Jesus emphasized that there are two kingdoms (Matthew 6:24) and two categories of treasures (Matthew 6:19-20). One is vulnerable to loss, while the other is eternally secure.

CONFEDERATE CASH

Between the first cannon shot on April 12, 1861, at Fort Sumter, South Carolina, and the Appomattox Courthouse on April 9, 1865, where Lee surrendered to Grant, the Confederacy printed their own currency and managed an independent economy. On April 10th, every Confederate dollar became functionally worthless.

Imagine what will happen to all the gold bullion, stocks, bonds, and cash in the world one moment after Jesus returns. As you calculate the value, recall that gold is used in place of asphalt in heaven (Revelation 21:21).

There is still time for you to switch your investment strategy. Stop hoarding Confederate cash! Put it to work for the kingdom now, and start building your heavenly portfolio. Little or large, no giving in Jesus' name will go unrewarded. The Lord will remain a debtor to no man.

"For whoever gives you a cup of water to drink in My name, because you belong to Christ, assuredly, I say to you, he will by no means lose his reward." (Mark 9:41)

THE TREASURE PRINCIPLE

Randy Alcorn's bestselling book *The Treasure Principle* was based on the fact that it is possible to store up heavenly wealth in advance.

Jesus said to him, "If you want to be perfect, go, sell what you have and give to the poor, and you will have treasure in heaven; and come, follow Me." (Matthew 19:21)

Alcorn's short but potent book was published at the turn of the century and the millions of copies in circulation have certainly helped revolutionize the giving philosophy of many believers. I suspect that those who are wisely following his guidelines for the secret of joyful giving will thank him in heaven—just as someone would an investment broker who advised them to buy Apple stock in the early 1980s.

The mere fact that it is totally possible to take action now and reap the rewards in eternity should make your head snap to attention. At the very least you should thoroughly investigate how you could be preparing right now for your experience in eternity. After all, earthly investment strategies speak of wise living in the present to ensure comfort 30 years from now.

The Treasure Principle counsels how we can impact our lives 30 million years from now.

CLASSIC INVENTORY OUTLINE

There is no clear record of who first said this, but they nailed it, "Time, talent, and treasure—these three are the currency we can invest in God's Kingdom." True wisdom.

The Bible is clear that our giving should be prayerful, private, and joyous. Giving grudgingly is not true giving at all, and neither is the gift designed to attract attention to the giver.

"Therefore, when you do a charitable deed, do not sound a trumpet before you as the hypocrites do in the synagogues and in the streets, that they may have glory from men. Assuredly, I say to you, they have their reward." (Matthew 6:2)

ECONOMY OF THE KINGDOM

Just as we are familiar with Wall Street, Dow Jones, and wise retirement strategies in this life, we should also understand the economy in God's kingdom. Scripture dictates that our willful investment in what Jesus called "the Father's business" will be handsomely rewarded (Luke 2:49).

We should do our research before we make our investments.

Blue-chip stocks, from a spiritual standpoint, would be investing in the church because this is the only institution that will survive and exist in the next life. The church is also near and dear to the heart of God. You cannot miss by giving to a true New Testament church. In fact, this should be a cornerstone of your portfolio.

If you view heaven as a corporation, God would be the CEO. Therefore, it would be wise to understand His passions for charity. Jesus said His sheep would give to widows, visit prisoners, and help the needy. Let's consider those investments to be super solid utility stocks. The need will always be there and so will the commendation of our Lord—a dependable return on our investment.

To take this investment analogy one step further, part of your endowments should include the equivalent of new ventures, what is known as an IPO, or initial public offerings. These startups can pay handsome dividends, but they are not without risk.

In our spiritual context, these stocks would be church plants, new missionaries, or entrepreneurial charities such as Fresh Water Ministries (see FWM.World for more information). Do your homework, take the plunge, and then experience the joy of seeing your investments produce fruit.

WHAT AND WHY

How to invest in eternity is the easy part. Making sure our hearts are in the right place can be more difficult to ascertain.

Here is a quick investment seminar to help. Consider these four questions that reveal motives:

- What do you value most?
- What would you hate to lose most?
- What occupies your thought life?
- What brings you the most pleasure in life?

Martin Luther said, "I have held many things in my hands and I have lost them all. But the things I placed in God's hands I still possess."[4]

God is obviously not interested in the riches of man. He has created endless wealth. What is of interest to Him is the heart. He is focused on the devotion and passion of those in His church.

You do not want to arrive in heaven empty-handed, saved but singed by a fire—the same fire that burned up all your works just like wood, hay, and stubble (1 Corinthians 3:12). So, what is in your spiritual portfolio? Wise living now will ensure you are prepared to meet your God.

Be sure you know Jesus and the peace His forgiveness brings. After you've taken care of that, move on to the next task, which is to serve Him wholeheartedly. From this moment until the day you see Him face to face, let your light shine so that you glorify God.

Keep in mind, you have a fixed appointment with the most important Person in the universe. You will not be late for it. The question is, will you be prepared to meet your Maker?

As the wonderful gospel hymn advises, "People Get Ready."

Those who are wise shall shine

Like the brightness of the firmament,

And those who turn many to righteousness

Like the stars forever and ever. (Daniel 12:3)

26

THE UNVEILING

Revelation 22

"The big question is, are you ready? If you have never repented of your sins and by faith in Jesus' resurrection invited Him into your heart, please do so immediately. ... If you are already a Christian, let me ask you a question: Are you ready for Jesus' return?" – Tim LaHaye[1]

Now, John is shown a river of life (vv. 1–5). It is symbolic of the life flowing from God, the creator of life (Psalm 46:4–7).

On both sides of this river John sees the tree(s) of life, lining the river. The leaves of the trees are for the healing of nations. With no sickness in new Jerusalem, the meaning here is symbolic, as with the river. The leaves represent the healing God has brought to the nations, by virtue of the cross, which is God's redemptive tree of life. Through the cross, Christ nullified the curse (v. 3) and redeemed us from it, having become a curse for us (Galatians 3:13–14).

We will see His face, the face of Christ. For God is spirit, and the Holy Spirit's ministry will have ended. Notice in verses 3 through 5, where the throne of God and the Lamb reside, there is no darkness (night). Rather, we find four attributes of our relationship with Christ: service, intimacy, identity, and light.

The prophecies (v. 6) regarding things to come are not for a select few, but for all of God's people. In fact, Jesus said there is a blessing for all who keep the prophecy of this book of Revelation (v. 7). This is precisely why the devil has sought to keep believers from this book.

In verses 8 and 9, the angel has to rebuke John again and remind him to worship God. This brings us hope as we recognize that even John had to be reminded to forsake distractions and keep the focus on the main thing.

The return of Christ will happen suddenly. In whatever state He finds each person, that is how they will continue (v. 11). The time for decision will have passed. Just as the hand of God Himself shut the entrance to the ark of Noah, this holy moment brings a close to the door of grace.

We also find a testimony of warning and a promise.

First, Christ's testimony as our Messiah (vv. 16-17). Jesus is that bright morning star, the hope of the world, and the splendor and glory of His kingdom. This is the message of the Spirit and the bride.

Secondly, John issues a stern warning to all who hear the words of this book (vv. 18-19). What does the phrase "God will take away His part" in verse 19 mean? The idea here is that those who do not keep His word, but rather seek to delete or add to His word (and the book of Revelation in particular) actually have no faith in His word. They have no faith to save them. Therefore, their names will be blotted out from the Book of Life.

Finally, we find a powerful promise when John ends on a note of grace: "Even so, come, Lord Jesus" (v. 20). Oh, how sweet the sound. These things will come to pass, and very soon we will see His face.

REFERENCES & NOTES

INTRODUCTION

1. Joel Rosenberg, "Pandemics, Plagues and Promises," Audio Interview, March 2020, Connection Communication.

1. THE REVELATION OF JESUS CHRIST

1. Martin Lloyd-Jones, *True Happiness* (Wheaton: Crossway, 2001), 88.
2. Eugene Peterson, *Reversed Thunder* (New York: HarperCollins), xi, xii.

2. BLESSED FOR SUCCESS PART 1: EPHESUS

1. David Jeremiah, *Escape the Coming Night* (Nashville: Thomas Nelson), 48.

3. BLESSED FOR SUCCESS PART 2: SMYRNA

1. F. B. Meyer, *Steps into the Blessed Life* (Philadelphia: Henry Altemus), 150.
2. John MacArthur, "Bewitched by False Doctrine," August 20, 2017.

4. BLESSED FOR SUCCESS PART 3: PERGAMOS

1. John MacArthur, "The Lord's Word to His Church," September 6, 2015.
2. Billy Graham, Quoted in Franklin Graham, *Billy Graham in Quotes* (Nashville: Thomas Nelson), 86.
3. Graham, *Billy Graham*, 75.
4. "Christian Persecution," OpenDoors USA, n.d.
5. Beth Ross and Emma Rogers, "5 Quotes from Persecuted Christians," January 24, 2017.

5. BLESSED FOR SUCCESS PART 4: THYATIRA

1. James Dobson, *Life on the Edge* (Carol Stream: Tyndale House).
2. Pure Hope, "Statistics," 2020, https://purehope.net/resources/statistics/.
3. Joseph Seiss, *The Letters of Jesus* (Philadelphia: Lutheran Publication House).
4. James Clear, *Atomic Habits* (New York: Avery), 37.
5. John R. W. Stott, *What Christ Thinks of the Church*, 78.

6. BLESSED FOR SUCCESS PART 5: SARDIS

1. Timothy Keller, GoodReads Timothy J. Keller Quotes, n.d.
2. A. W. Tozer, GoodReads A. W. Tozer Quotes, n.d.

7. BLESSED FOR SUCCESS PART 6: PHILADELPHIA

1. Dan DeHaan, *The God You Can Know* (Chicago: Moody).
2. Jeremiah, *Escape*, 85.
3. Danniebelle Hall, "Ordinary People," by John Stephens, BMG Rights Management, Sony/ATV Music Publishing LLC, Royalty Network.

8. BLESSED FOR SUCCESS PART 7: LAODICEA

1. Francis Chan, *Crazy Love*.
2. Mark Wilson, *Biblical Turkey*, 253.

9. THE HEAVENLY VISION

1. C. S. Lewis, *Mere Christianity* (New York: HarperCollins), 134.
2. "When in Doubt, Shout It Out! 8 Drug-Free Ways to Battle Anxiety" Healthline, n.d.

10. PREVIEW OF COMING ATTRACTIONS

1. Chuck Smith, AZQuotes, n.d.
2. Andrew Fitzgerald, "10 Terrible Famines in History," Listverse, April 10, 2013.
3. Linda Lowry, "11 Christians Killed Every Day for Their Decision to Follow Jesus," OpenDoors USA, March 13, 2019.

4. Eric Hobsbawm, "War and Peace," February 22, 2002.
5. Courses of Western Civilization II, Lumen Learning.
6. John Walters, "Communism Killed 94M in 20th Century, Feels Need to Kill Again," March 13, 2013.
7. Billy Graham, billygraham.org, January 18, 2008.

11. REMNANT OF MERCY

1. Jeff Lasseigne, *Unlocking the Last Days* (Grand Rapids: Baker Books), 113.
2. Leo Tolstoy, "What is the Jew?"
3. Tom Lehrer, "National Brotherhood Week"
4. *Fiddler on the Roof*, directed by Norman Jewison (1971; The Mirisch Production Company).
5. Lisa Katz, "Jewish Accomplishments," Updated July 4, 2017.
6. Mark Twain, "Concerning the Jews," *Harper's Magazine*.
7. Eric Cline, "Do We Divide the Holiest Holy City?" *Moment Magazine*

12. DELAYED JUDGMENT RELEASED

1. Joel Rosenberg, *What the Bible Teaches about Pandemics*, 11, 12.
2. Mike Berardino, "Mike Tyson Explains One of His Most Famous Quotes," November 9, 2012
3. Joel Rosenberg, "What Does the Bible Teach," 2.
4. Hillary Johnson, "Killer Flu," January 22, 1998.
5. Edmond Hooker, "Biological Warfare," Reviewed January 10, 2019.
6. Dr. Steven Collins, Dr. LaTayne C. Scott, *Discovering the City of Sodom*
7. Phillip J. Silvia Ph.D., *The Destruction of Sodom*

13. THE DEFIANT ONES

1. Skip Heitzig, *You Can Understand the Book of Revelation*, 99.

14. ETERNAL WITNESSES

1. Dave Hunt, *A Cup of Trembling*, 343.
2. Walter Scott, *Exposition of the Revelation of Jesus Christ*, 223.
3. Don Stewart and Chuck Missler, *The Coming Temple*, 15.
4. Joel Rosenberg, *Epicenter*, 191.
5. Stewart and Missler, *The Coming*, 54.

6. AFP, "Top Iran General Says Destroying Israel 'Achievable Goal,'" September 30, 2019.

15. THE OVERCOMERS

1. John Walvoord, *Revelation*, 197.
2. Geeta Pandey, "Indian man to sue parents for giving birth to him," BBC, February 7, 2019.

16. MANIFESTATION OF THE BEAST

1. Tim LaHaye, in *When the Trumpet Sounds,* ed. Thomas Ice, 437.
2. Thomas Cahill, *The Gifts of the Jews,* 3.
3. H. A. Ironside, *Lectures on the Book of Revelation.*
4. Merril Unger, *Biblical Demonology,* 197.
5. John MacArthur, "The Rise and Fall of the World, Part 1," November 25, 1979.
6. LaHaye, in *When the Trumpet,* ed. Thomas Ice, 431.
7. Goodreads, "A Quote by Alexander Fraser Tytler," Goodreads, August 7, 2020.

17. GRAPES OF WRATH

1. Heitzig, *You Can Understand,* 143.

18. THE FINALITY OF DIVINE WRATH

1. J. C. Ryle, 159.

19. THE SCARLET HARLOT

1. J. Dwight Pentecost, *Things to Come,* 369.
2. Jay Michaelson, "United Methodist Denomination Votes to Expel LGBT Pastors and Pro-LGBT Churches," Updated February 27, 2019.

20. BABYLON IS FALLEN

1. Robert Gromacki, in *When the Trumpet Sounds*, ed. Thomas Ice, 353.

21. ENTER THE LION

1. St. Augustine, GoodReads Augustine of Hippo Quotes, n.d.
2. "The Knot 2019 Real Weddings Study," The Knot, n.d.
3. "Most Expensive Weddings of All Time," CBS News, n.d.
4. Kevin Howard and Marvin Rosenthal, *The Feasts of the Lord*, 14.

22. JUDGMENT DAY!

1. Levi Lusko, "Through the Eyes of a Lion," March 21, 2017.
2. Anthony DeStefano, *Hell: A Guide*, 26.
3. DeStefano, *Hell*, 24.
4. DeStefano, *Hell*, 159.
5. Rob Bell, *Love Wins*, 109.
6. Ted Turner, Famous Quote From, n.d.
7. *Crimes and Misdemeanors*, directed by Woody Allen (1989; Orion Pictures).
8. Richard Neuhaus, in Larry Dixon, *The Other Side of the Good News*, 25.
9. Jonathan Edwards, "Sinners in the Hands of an Angry God," July 8, 1741.
10. John MacArthur, SermonQuotes, n.d.
11. Edwards, "Sinners," July 8, 1741.
12. Dante Alighieri, *Inferno*.
13. C. S. Lewis, *The Great Divorce*, 66, 67
14. Charles Spurgeon, cited by Edward Fudge, "Putting Hell in Its Place," August 6, 1976.
15. Lasseigne, *Unlocking*, 281.

23. A GLIMPSE OF ETERNAL GLORY

1. Charles Spurgeon, GoodReads Charles Hadden Spurgeon Quotes, n.d.
2. Randy Alcorn, *Heaven*, xix.
3. J. C. Ryle, *Heaven*, 19.
4. Bart Millard, "I Can Only Imagine," 2001.
5. Alcorn, *Heaven*, 20.
6. Chuck Missler, "The Realm of Angels," 2012.
7. Michael T. Nappier, quoted in "8 Dog Nose Facts You Probably Didn't Know," December 21, 2016.

8. Max Lucado, *Just Like Jesus.*

24. ALTERNATIVE ENDINGS

1. C.S. Lewis, GoodReads C. S. Lewis Quotes, n.d.
2. Randy Alcorn, *The Treasure Principle.*
3. Bob Goff, GoodReads Bob Goff Quotes, n.d.
4. Based on the closing price of AAPL on 8/10/2020, the market capitalization is 1.928 trillion.
5. Paul Billheimer, *Destined for the Throne.*

25. PREPARE TO MEET THY GOD

1. C. S. Lewis, *The Weight of Glory.*
2. George Muller, "An Abundant Entrance," GeorgeMuller.org, posted December 12, 2016.
3. Randy Alcorn, *Money, Possessions, and Eternity.*
4. Martin Luther, GoodReads Martin Luther Quotes, n.d.

26. THE UNVEILING

1. LaHaye, in *When the Trumpet*, ed. Thomas Ice, 443, 444

ABOUT THE AUTHOR

Al Pittman is the Senior Pastor of Calvary Worship Center in Colorado Springs, Colorado. He was born in Panama City, Florida in 1955. His father was a career soldier, so the family traveled extensively. In 1973, when Al was seventeen years old, the family returned from a tour in Germany and settled in Colorado Springs. Soon after, Al realized God's call on his life and began serving in the music ministry as a bass guitarist with a Christian band called *The Rays of Light*. It was during this time that Al met Norma, and they were married on July 19, 1975.

Al attended Nazarene Bible College in Colorado Springs, graduating in 1977 with a degree in Biblical Studies. Several years later he visited Calvary Chapel, which had opened across the street from where he worked. After attending one service, he was hooked, rejoicing to be taught the Word of God. He couldn't get enough and became involved in the worship band at Calvary Chapel, as well as performing with a local contemporary Christian band. In 1980, the Lord granted Al the privilege of becoming a full-time staff member with Calvary Chapel of Colorado Springs, where he conducted Friday evening outreach concerts along with other pastoral duties assigned to him. In 1991 Al and his family moved to Albuquerque, New Mexico, and two years later he joined the staff of Calvary Church Albuquerque as an assistant pastor and co-worship leader.

In the spring of 1997, the Lord called Al and his family back to Colorado Springs to pastor Calvary Worship Center. Although this was a difficult decision, they knew the Lord was leading them, and they have seen and experienced God's awesome faithfulness since returning to Colorado Springs, where the fellowship has grown along with their faith. In 2006, Al earned his Master's degree and in 2012 he earned his Doctorate degree in Ministry from Trinity Southwest University in Albuquerque, New Mexico. Al and Norma are the proud parents of three children, Renee, Nathan, and Reggie, as well as proud grandparents. They covet your prayers for their family and ministry as they endeavor to live a life pleasing to the Father. To God be the glory for all He has done and all He will do!